Windows 98 Cheat Sheet

by Shelley O'Hara

A Division of Macmillan Computer Publishing
201 W. 103rd Street, Indianapolis, Indiana 46290 USA

International Standard Book Number: 0-7897-1901-0

Library of Congress Catalog Card Number: 98-87537

Printed in the United States of America

First Printing: March 1999

01   00   4

Trademarks

Warning and Disclaimer

Executive Editor:	*Christopher Will*
Development Editor	*Kate Shoup Welsh*
Managing Editor	*Brice Gosnell*
Project Editor	*Katie Purdum*
Copy Editor	*Kate Givens*
Proofreader	*Jennifer Earhart*
Indexer	*Heather Goens*
Technical Editor	*Vince Averello*
Production	*Tim Osborn*
	Staci Somers

Table of Contents

Part I Getting Started   1

1 Starting and Shutting Down Windows   3

Turning On the PC   3
Shutting Down the PC   4
Restarting the PC   4
What to Do If Nothing Happens When You Turn On the PC   5
What to Do If You Don't See the Windows Desktop   5
What to Do If You Can't Restart from the Start Menu   6

2 Understanding the Desktop   9

Desktop Icons   9
The Start Button   10
The Taskbar   11

3 Selecting a Command   13

Selecting Commands from the Start Menu   13
Selecting Commands in a Program   14
Using a Dialog Box   14
Selecting a Program Command from the Keyboard   16
Using a Shortcut Menu   16

4 Working with Windows   19

Opening a Window   19
Closing a Window   20
Resizing a Window   20
Moving a Window   21
Arranging Open Windows   21

5 Working with Icons   23

Understanding Types of Icons   23
Moving Icons   24
Arranging Icons   24
Lining Up Icons   25

6 Getting Help   **27**

Using Help Contents   27

Using the Help Index   28

Searching for a Help Topic   29

Part II Working with Programs   31

7 Starting a Program   **33**

Starting a Program   33

Exiting a Program   34

Starting a Program and Opening a Document   34

Starting a Program with a Shortcut Icon   35

Starting a Program with a Shortcut Icon   36

Starting a Program Each Time You Start Windows   36

8 Switching Among Programs   **39**

Switching Among Programs   39

Using the Keyboard to Switch   39

Minimizing All Programs (and Windows)   40

9 Installing and Uninstalling New Programs   **43**

Purchasing a New Program   43

Installing a New Program   44

Uninstalling a Program   46

Using the Run Command to Install a Program   47

Adding Windows Components   47

10 Setting Up the Start Menu   **51**

Deleting Programs on the Start Menu   53

Adding Folders to the Start Menu   54

Rearranging the Start Menu   55

11 Creating Shortcuts   **57**

Creating a Shortcut   57

Deleting a Shortcut Icon   58

Renaming a Shortcut Icon   58

12 Selecting Text   **61**

Selecting Text   61

Selecting Text with the Keyboard   62

Selecting a Range in a Worksheet   62

13 Copying and Moving Text   **65**

    Deleting Text   65

    Moving Text   65

    Copying Text   67

    Copying to Another Program   68

14 Saving a Document   **71**

    Saving a Document the First Time   71

    Saving a Document Again   72

    Saving a Document with Another Name   72

    Saving a Document As Another File Type   73

15 Opening a Document   **75**

    Opening a Document   75

    Switching Among Open Documents   76

    Displaying All Open Documents   77

16 Closing a Document and Creating a New Document   **79**

    Closing a Document   79

    Creating a New Document   79

    Using a Template   80

17 Printing a Document   **83**

    Printing a Document   83

    Previewing a Document   84

    Setting Up a Document Page   84

Part III Using Windows Accessories   **87**

18 Creating Documents with WordPad   **89**

    Starting WordPad and Typing Text   89

    Editing Text   90

    Formatting Text   90

    Formatting Paragraphs   91

    Formatting Pages   92

19 Creating Pictures with Paint   **95**

    Starting Paint   95

    Using the Toolbox   95

    Drawing an Object   97

    Erasing Part of a Drawing   98

Filling an Object with Color   99
Copying an Object   100

20 Playing Sounds and Movies   **103**
Playing Music   103
Playing Sounds   104
Playing Media Clips and Movies   105
Playing a Different Track on a CD   106
Recording Sounds   107

21 Sending and Receiving Faxes   **111**
Sending a Fax   111
Receiving and Viewing a Fax   113
Dialing Your Phone with Phone Dialer   114

22 Playing Games   **117**
Playing Solitaire   117
Playing Hearts   118
Playing FreeCell   118
Playing Minesweeper   119

23 Doing Calculations with Calculator   **121**
Figuring a Calculation   121
Using the Clear and Memory Buttons   122
Changing the Calculator   122

24 Editing Text Files with Notepad   **125**
Creating a Text File   125
Opening and Editing a Text File   126
Searching for Text in a Text File   127

Part IV Managing Files   129

25 Displaying Files and Folders   **129**
Using My Computer to Display Files   131
Changing the View   132
Sorting the Contents   133
Using Windows Explorer   134
Working in Web View   135

26 Creating New Folders **139**

Creating a New Folder 139

Renaming a Folder 140

Deleting a Folder 140

Moving Folders 141

Copying Folders 142

27 Selecting Files **145**

Selecting and Deselecting a File 145

Selecting Several Files 145

Inverting a Selection 147

28 Moving and Copying Files **149**

Moving Files 149

Copying Files from One Folder to Another 150

Copying Files from Your Hard Disk to a Floppy Disk 151

Moving Files with a Command 152

Copying Files with a Command 152

29 Deleting and Undeleting Files **155**

Deleting a File 155

Undeleting a File 156

Emptying the Recycle Bin 156

30 Renaming Files or Folders **159**

Renaming a File 159

Decoding Filenames 160

31 Searching for Files **163**

Searching for a File or Folder by Name 163

Searching for a File or Folder by Contents 164

Finding Files and Folders by Date 166

32 Displaying Disk Properties **169**

Displaying File Properties 169

Displaying Folder Properties 170

Displaying Disk Properties 171

Viewing System Properties 171

Part V   Customizing Windows   173

33 Changing How the Desktop Looks   **175**

   Wall-papering Your Desktop   175
   Using a Pattern   176
   Using a Different Color Scheme   177
   Changing How the Icons Are Displayed   177
   Changing the Screen Area   178
   Using Another File for the Wallpaper   179
   Editing the Pattern   180
   Changing Individual Colors   181

34 Using a Screen Saver   **185**

   Using a Screen Saver   185
   Using a Password   186
   Changing Screen Saver Options   187

35 Viewing Your Desktop as a Web Page   **191**

   Viewing Active Desktop   191
   Viewing Channels   192

36 Changing the Taskbar   **197**

   Moving the Taskbar   197
   Resizing the Taskbar   198
   Selecting Taskbar Options   198

37 Changing the System Date and Time   **201**

   Changing the Date and Time   201
   Changing the Date and Time   202
   Changing Regional Settings   202

38 Customizing the Mouse   **205**

   Switching Mouse Buttons   205
   Custom-izing the Keyboard   206
   Using Different Mouse Pointers   207
   Changing the Pointer Speed and Adding a Pointer Trail   207

39 Playing a Sound for Windows Events   **211**

   Assigning a Sound to an Action   211
   Using a Sound Scheme   212

40 Configuring Windows for Special Needs   **215**

   Turning On Accessibility Options   215
   Customizing Accessibility Options   217

Part VI Maintaining Your System 219

41 Checking for Errors   **221**

    Running ScanDisk   221

    Setting ScanDisk Options   223

42 Defragmenting Your Disks   **225**

    Defragmenting Your Hard Drive   226

    Viewing the Defragmenting Progress   227

43 Cleaning Up Files   **229**

    Cleaning Up Your Disk   229

    Setting Other Cleanup Options   230

44 Creating a Startup Disk   **233**

    Formatting a Floppy Disk   233

    Creating a Startup Disk   234

45 Backing Up Your System   **237**

    Backing Up All Files   237

    Speeding Up the Backup Process   238

    Backing Up Selected Files   239

46 Restoring a Backup   **243**

    Restoring Files   243

47 Setting Up Your Printer   **249**

    Installing a New Printer   249

    Handling Print Jobs   251

    Setting the Default Printer   252

    Installing New Hardware   255

    Plug and Play Setup   255

    Running the Hardware Wizard   256

48 Scheduling Tasks   **259**

    Adding a Task   259

    Deleting a Scheduled Task   261

    Modifying a Scheduled Task   261

49 Troubleshooting Problems   **265**

    Running the Device Manager   265

    Avoiding Viruses   267

    Scanning Your PC With an Anti-Virus Program   267

VII Connecting to the Internet 271

50 Getting Connected to the Internet   **273**

What You Need To Get Connected   273

Setting Up for the Internet   274

Making Changes to the Setup   279

51 Starting and Exiting Internet Explorer   **281**

Logging On   281

Logging Off   282

Changing Your Connection Settings   282

52 Browsing the Internet   **285**

Clicking Links To Browse   285

Typing an Address   286

Using Toolbar Buttons   287

Adding a Site to Your Favorites List   287

Going to a Site in Your Favorites List   288

Using the History List   289

53 Searching the Internet   **291**

Searching the Internet   291

Using a Different Search Tool   292

Browsing a Search Directory   293

54 Sending and Receiving Email   **295**

Starting Your Email Program   295

Understanding Your Email Address   296

Checking Your Mail   297

Responding to Mail   297

Sending New Mail   298

Handling Mail   299

55 Joining Newsgroups   **301**

Subscribing to Newsgroups   301

Reading Newsgroup Messages   302

Replying to a Message   304

Posting a New Message   305

About the Author

Shelley O'Hara works as a freelance writer in Indianapolis. She is the author of over 70 books, including several best-selling titles. She wrote the original Easy series, and the new editions of *Easy Windows 95* and *Easy Windows 98*. O'Hara also does training for the Division of Continuing Studies for Indiana University and Purdue University at Indianapolis. She graduated with a BA in English from the University of South Carolina and also has an MA in English from the University of Maryland.

Dedication

To my Florida tennis buddies: Shawna, Lyn, and Michelle.

Acknowledgments

Hats off to Kate Welsh, for her usual superb editing job. Also, thanks to Chris Will for inviting me to do this project and to Vince Averello for his technical review.

Tell Us What You Think!

As the reader of this book, *you* are our most important critic and commentator. We value your opinion and want to know what we're doing right, what we could do better, what areas you'd like to see us publish in, and any other words of wisdom you're willing to pass our way.

As the Executive Editor for the [Web development] team at Macmillan Computer Publishing, I welcome your comments. You can fax, email, or write me directly to let me know what you did or didn't like about this book—as well as what we can do to make our books stronger.

Please note that I cannot help you with technical problems related to the topic of this book, and that due to the high volume of mail I receive, I might not be able to reply to every message.

When you write, please be sure to include this book's title and author, as well as your name and phone or fax number. I will carefully review your comments and share them with the author and editors who worked on the book.

Fax: 317-817-7070

Email: opsys@mcp.com

Mail: Chris Will
         Executive Editor
         Operating Systems
         Macmillan Computer Publishing
         201 West 103rd Street
         Indianapolis, IN 46290 USA

Introduction

Using Windows is supposed to make things easier, but you may not have time to wade through a big, fat manual to find the information you need. You need to know just the basics, just the stuff to get by in your day-to-day work. You need a cheat sheet. And that's this book.

What Makes This Book Different

This book is designed to make using a computer as easy as possible, weeding out extraneous information and focusing on the skills you need to use Windows most effectively. Here are the key benefits of this book:

- The key concepts are highlighted, helping you identify the most important information.

- This book doesn't cover each and every feature; it covers the features you are most likely to use and will get the most benefit from.

- This book is divided into 60 or so short sections that deal with a particular topic. Finding the information you need is easy.

- Each chapter starts with a Cheat Sheet—a quick list of the most important information and steps in the chapter.

- Within each chapter, the most basic tasks are covered first in a section called "Basic Survival." When you are just getting started, concentrate on these sections.

- After the "Basic Survival" section, you'll find a "Beyond Survival" section, which covers the topic in a little more detail. Check out these sections when you want to learn more about a topic.

- For every task, you will find step-by-step instructions, illustrated with figures so that you can easily follow along.

How This Book Is Organized

This book is organized into several parts:

- Part I, "Getting Started," covers the basic information about using Windows—how to start and exit Windows, select menu commands, work with windows, and more.

- Part II, "Working with Programs," explains all you need to know to get started using most programs. You not only learn how to start programs, but also some key skills that work from one program to the next.

- Part III, "Using Windows Accessories," explains how to use the mini-programs (called accessories) included with Windows 98. You learn how to create documents with WordPad, pictures with Paint, text files with Notepad, and more.

- Part IV, "Managing Files," describes how to manage the files on your computer. You can find information on how to copy, rename, delete, and otherwise handle the files on your system.

- Part V, "Customizing Windows," covers some of the different ways you can change how your PC works. You can find features that will make your work easier or simply more pleasing to you.

- Part VI, "Maintaining Your PC," focuses on some tasks that you might not do every day, but should do every now and then. You find out how to check your hard drive for errors, back up important files, install new hardware, and more.

- Part VII, "Getting Connected to the Internet," takes you beyond your own computer to the wide world of the Internet. You learn what you need to get connected as well as what you can do once connected.

PART

1

Getting Started

To get started using Windows 98, you need a few basic skills, as covered in this section. Here you learn the tasks needed to work with icons on the desktop, select commands, get help, and more. The following topics are covered:

- Starting and Shutting Down Windows

- Understanding the Windows Desktop

- Selecting Commands

- Working with Windows

- Working with Icons

- Getting Help

Cheat Sheet

Starting Windows

1. Turn on your PC. Windows starts automatically.

Shutting Down Windows

1. Click the Start button.

2. Select the Shut Down command.

3. Select Shut down.

4. Click the OK button.

Restarting Windows

1. Click the Start button and select Shut Down.

2. Select Restart.

3. Click the OK button.

Starting and Shutting Down Windows

Starting Windows is as simple as flipping the power switch. Turning off the PC isn't quite as simple, though; you need to use a special command to turn off the PC. Also, at might you might get "stuck"; when that happens, you'll need to know how to restart your computer.

Basic Survival

Turning On the PC

To start Windows and use your PC, you simply turn it on. You should see some information flash across the screen as your system goes through its startup routine. For instance, you might see the results of a memory check. You might see setup commands for your hardware. After the system starts up, you should see the Windows 98 desktop.

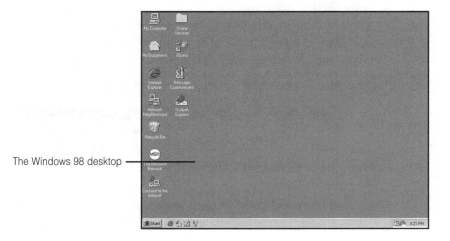

The Windows 98 desktop

Shutting Down the PC

Windows takes care of all the background details of using your PC—such things as storing files and handling the printer. Because the PC is often busy in the background, you shouldn't just turn it off. Instead, use the proper shutdown procedure so that Windows can take care of any housekeeping tasks before turning off the power.

Follow these steps to shut off your PC properly:

1. Click the Start button and select Shut Down. You see the Shut Down Windows dialog box.

2. Select Shut down.

Click this option button to shut down Windows 98

3. Click the OK button.

When you see a message saying that it is safe to turn off your PC, you can turn it off. Or your PC might turn off by itself.

Restarting the PC

Using a PC isn't error-proof. Sometimes things happen that make the PC freeze up. For instance, a program might crash. When this happens, pressing the keys does nothing. The PC just won't respond. In this case, you can restart your PC. You might also need to restart if you make changes to your system.

If your system won't respond, check a few things:

* Check to see whether the disk activity light is blinking. You can find this button on the front of the PC. If the light is blinking or you hear sounds, the PC might be busy saving a file or handling some other activity. Wait a few minutes.

* Be sure you know where you are. It's easy to switch to a different program, say back to the Windows desktop, without intending to. Although you think you are typing in your word processing program, you are really back at the desktop, and Windows doesn't understand all that

typing. Try clicking in the program window or using the taskbar to make sure that you are in the program you think you are.

- Check the screen. As another example, you might have opened a menu or dialog box without realizing it. Again, if you try typing, all you might hear are beeps. Try pressing Esc (the Escape key) to close any open menus or dialog boxes.

If all else fails, you can restart your PC:

1. Click the Start button and select Shut Down. You see the Shut Down Windows dialog box.

2. Select Restart.

3. Click the OK button.

Beyond Survival

What to Do If Nothing Happens When You Turn On the PC

If nothing happens when you turn on your PC, check the following:

- Do both the PC and the monitor have power?

- Are all the components connected?

- Did you turn on both the monitor and the PC? They have separate power buttons.

- Do you need to adjust the monitor? The monitor includes buttons for controlling the brightness of the display. It's easy to think the monitor isn't working when in fact you just can't see anything because of the brightness or other settings. Check these controls.

What to Do If You Don't See the Windows Desktop

It's more than likely that you have Windows 95 or 98 on your PC, but if you don't see the Windows desktop shown in the preceding section, your system might have a different setup.

One possibility is that you might have another desktop manager working on top of Windows. Sometimes PC manufacturers add a layer over Windows (a shell that runs on top of

5

Windows), with its own set of windows and controls and icons for using the PC. Each setup is different, so you can't ask others for help or really use a general-purpose book like this one. If this is the case, I'd recommend looking in your system documentation and figuring out how to turn off the desktop manager and just use Windows. Usually the shell is loaded from the Startup menu, and you can disable it by removing it from this folder.

What to Do If You Can't Restart from the Start Menu

If you can't click to get the Start menu open, you have to use a different method to restart. Try the keyboard method: Press and hold down the Ctrl key. Then press Alt and Delete at the same time. You often see this abbreviated as Ctrl+Alt+Delete. You see the Close Program dialog box. Select the program to close, and click End Task. Or click the Shut Down button.

If the keyboard method doesn't work, press the Reset button on the front of the PC. If that doesn't work or if you don't have a Reset button, try turning the PC off and then on.

Cheat Sheet

Icon —

Start button —

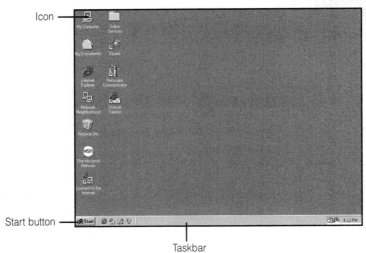

Taskbar

Understanding the Desktop

When you start your PC, you see the Windows desktop. This is always your starting place, and like your physical desktop, the Windows desktop includes several tools to get you started. Each of these items is placed on the desktop (the background area).

Basic Survival

Desktop Icons

You can place different items on the desktop so that they are always available. Each item is represented by a little picture called an icon. (You learn more about adding items to the desktop in Chapter 11, "Creating Shortcuts.") Windows includes several icons by default.

The My Computer icon is used to display the contents of your PC. You learn more about using this icon in Chapter 25, "Displaying Files and Folders"

The Recycle Bin is used to store files, folders, and programs you have deleted. You can double-click the icon to see the contents of this system folder. Chapter 29, "Deleting and Undeleting Files," explains all about deleting and undeleting files

See Chapter 5, "Working with Icons," in this part for information on moving and arranging icons.

You might have several other icons. For instance, if you are hooked up to a network, you might see the Network Neighborhood icon, which you can use to access and display the contents of the network. You might have icons for setting up MSN, a folder for online services, or an icon for your Inbox.

You might have icons you have added yourself. My desktop, for instance, includes icons for programs I frequently use.

The Start Button

Probably the most important item on the Windows desktop is the Start button. You use this button not only to start programs, but also to access most Windows features and commands.

To display the Start menu, click the Start button. You see the following choices:

The Start menu

- **Programs.** Use this command to start a program. Programs are organized into folders, displayed as submenus on the Programs menu. You learn more about starting programs in the Part II, "Working with Programs."

- **Favorites.** Use this command to access a list of folders and Internet Web sites you have added to your Favorites list.

- **Documents.** Use this command to open a document you recently worked on. This method for starting a program and opening a document is also covered in Part II.

- **Settings.** Use this command to access the Control Panel, Taskbar & Start Menu, and Printers folders, which you can use to set up and customize different Windows components. Customizing is the topic of Part V, "Customizing Windows."

- **Find.** Use this command to search for files and folders on the PC. Finding files is covered in Chapter 31, "Searching for Files."

- **Help.** Use this program to get online help, as covered in Chapter 6, "Getting Help."

- **Run.** Use this command to run programs, usually done for installing new programs. You can read about installing programs in Chapter 9, "Installing and Uninstalling New Programs."

- **Shut Down.** Use this command to shut down the computer before you turn off the power. Chapter 1, "Starting and Shutting Down Windows," explains how to perform this task. You can also restart using this command.

The Taskbar

The Start button is the first item in the taskbar, the horizontal bar along the bottom of the desktop. The taskbar also includes buttons for each window you have open or program you have running, which makes it easy for you to see what you have open. More important, the taskbar is what you use to switch among different programs.

If you work with more than one program, you might want to switch from one to another. Windows's taskbar makes switching easy. To switch to another program or window, simply click the button for that program or window in the taskbar. That program or window becomes active.

The taskbar also displays the current time, as well as status icons for different tasks such as printing and email, on the far right. Along the left part of the taskbar, you see the Quick Launch toolbar. You can use this toolbar to get connected to the Internet.

To display the current date, put the mouse pointer on the time.

You can change the placement and look of the taskbar. For more information on these changes, see Chapter 36, "Changing the Taskbar."

11

Cheat Sheet

Selecting Commands from the Start Menu

1. Click the Start button.

2. To display a submenu, put the pointer over the command you want to select. You can also click the command.

3. Continue selecting commands from submenus by pointing to them until you get to the selection you want.

4. Click your selection.

Selecting Commands in a Program

1. Click the menu you want to open.

2. Click the command.

3. If you see a submenu, click the command you want from this menu.

4. If you see a dialog box, make your selections and click the OK button.

Using a Dialog Box

- **Tab.** Click on the tab to see the options for that tab.
- **Text box.** Type the entry in the text box.
- **Spin box.** Type the value in the spin box, or click the spin arrows to scroll through the values.
- **List box.** Click the item you want from the list.
- **Drop-down list box.** Click the down arrow to display the list, and then click the item you want from this list.
- **Check box.** Click the box to turn on an item (checked) or turn off an option (unchecked).
- **Option button.** Click the button to turn on an item (darkened button) or turn off an option (blank button).
- **Command button.** Click the OK button to confirm your choices. Click Cancel to close the dialog box without carrying out the command.

3

Selecting a Command

Selecting commands is simple, and after you learn how to select a command in one program, you can use these same skills in any program. In Windows, you select commands from the Start menu or from a shortcut menu. This section also explains how to select commands from a program menu.

Basic Survival

Selecting Commands from the Start Menu

To select a command from the Start menu, follow these steps:

1. Click the Start button. You see the top-level menu commands.

2. To display a submenu, put the pointer over the command you want to select. You can also click the command. When the pointer is over a command with a submenu (indicated with an arrow), the submenu is displayed. Continue selecting commands from submenus by pointing to them until you get to the selection you want.

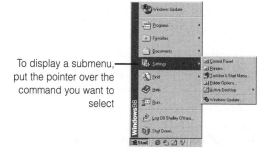

To display a submenu, put the pointer over the command you want to select

3. Click your selection.

The command is carried out. For instance, if you select a program icon, that program is started.

Selecting Commands in a Program

In most programs, the menu bar appears at the top of the screen. This bar lists the names of the menus, and you can click them to display a list of commands in each menu. To select a command from a program menu, follow these steps:

1. Click the name of the menu you want to open. You see a list of commands (here the File menu from Word for Windows).

Open a menu to see the available commands

2. Click the command.

For some commands, the command is carried out.

If you select a command that is followed by an arrow, you see a submenu. Click the command you want from this menu.

Press Esc to close a menu without making a selection.

If the command is followed by ellipses, you see a dialog box, which prompts you for additional information about how to carry out the command. Make your selections and click the OK button.

Using a Dialog Box

For some commands, the program needs additional information. For instance, when you print a document, you can specify the number of copies to print or which printer to use. In this case, the program displays a dialog box, with the available options for carrying out the command.

Every dialog box is different and contains different options, but they all work in a similar fashion. After you learn the basics of selecting each type of item, you are set. The following figures identify the different types of options, and the list explains how to select each type of option.

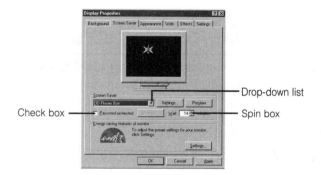

Check box ——— Drop-down list · Spin box

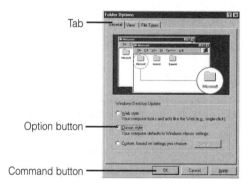

Tab
Option button
Command button

- **Tab.** Click on the tab to see the options for that tab.

- **Text box.** Type the entry in the text box.

- **Spin box.** Type the value in the spin box, or use the spin arrows to scroll through the values.

- **List box.** Click the item you want from the list.

- **Drop-down list box.** Click the down arrow to display the list, and then click the item you want from this list.

- **Check box.** Click the box to turn on an item (checked) or turn off an option (unchecked).

- **Option button.** Click the button to turn on an item (darkened button) or turn off an option (blank button).

- **Command button.** Click the OK button to confirm your choices. Click Cancel to close the dialog box without carrying out the command.

Beyond Survival

Selecting a Program Command from the Keyboard

If you prefer, you can use the keyboard to select a menu command. Some commands have shortcut keys; you can press this key or key combination to select the command. You can also open a menu and select a command using the keyboard. Follow these steps:

1. Press the Alt key to activate the menu bar.

2. Press the "key" letter of the menu. The key letter is underlined onscreen. For instance, press F to open the File menu. You often see steps 1 and 2 described as "press Alt+F."

3. Press the "key" letter for the command.

Using a Shortcut Menu

In addition to the main commands, you can often use shortcut menus. You can display these menus and select commands by using the right mouse button. Follow these steps:

1. Point to the item you want to work with. In Windows, you can display a shortcut menu for the desktop, the taskbar, icons, files, the time in the status bar, and other "hot" spots. You can also use shortcuts in other programs by clicking on the item or object you want to modify.

2. Click the right mouse button. A shortcut menu is displayed (shown here for the desktop).

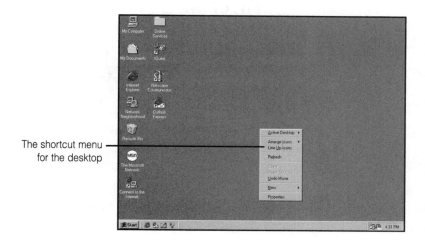

The shortcut menu
for the desktop

3. Click the command you want.

17

Cheat Sheet

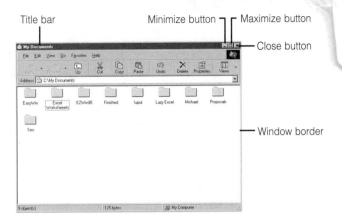

Title bar — Minimize button — Maximize button — Close button — Window border

4

Working with Windows

Everything in Windows is displayed in a window, and one of the key skills you need to learn is how to manipulate a window—that is, how to open, close, resize, and move a window.

Basic Survival

Opening a Window

Some windows display the contents of a disk or folder. For instance, the My Computer icon displays the contents of your system, and the Recycle Bin displays the contents of this folder. To open this type of window, double-click its icon. The window is displayed on the desktop, and you also see a button for the window in the taskbar.

Some windows display a program. To open this type of window, start the program. The program is started and displayed in a program window, and Windows adds a button for this program to the taskbar.

Both types of windows have the same set of controls.

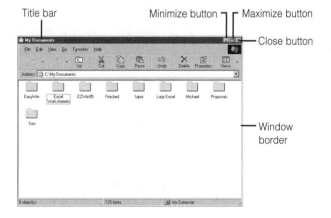

When you are working in a program, you actually have two windows open: the program window and the document window. Each has its own set of controls. The set in the title bar controls the program window. The set below this one (to the far right of the menu bar when the document window is maximized) controls the document window.

Closing a Window

To close a window, click the Close (×) button in the title bar. If you close a program window, you exit that program.

You can also close programs or windows by right-clicking the button for that program or window on the taskbar. From the shortcut menu, select the Close command.

Beyond Survival

Resizing a Window

You might have several windows open at the same time. To view them all, you might need to make some adjustments to the windows' sizes. You have a lot of options for resizing. You can use the buttons in the title bar, or you can drag the window borders. (To drag, click and hold down the mouse button, and then move the pointer.) For resizing, do any of the following:

- To minimize a window (shrink it to a button on the taskbar), click the Minimize button. When you minimize a window, that window or program is still running but is not displayed in a window.

- To maximize a window (expand it to fill the entire screen), click the Maximize button. When a window is maximized, the window does not have borders, so you cannot resize by dragging the borders. Also, the Maximize button becomes the Restore button.

- To restore a maximized window to its original size, click the Restore button.

- To resize a window, put the pointer on any of the window's borders, but not on the title bar. Drag the border to change the size of the window.

Moving a Window

If you have several windows open, you might also need to move windows around to see just what you want. You can move a window by following these steps:

1. Put the pointer on the title bar.

2. Drag the window to the location you want.

Arranging Open Windows

You can have Windows arrange all windows onscreen. To do so, follow these steps:

1. Right-click a blank area of the taskbar.

2. Select Cascade, Tile Horizontally, or Tile Vertically.

Cascade displays the windows on top of each other; you can see the title bar of each window (shown in the following figure). Tile Horizontally displays each window a in horizontal pane. Tile Vertically displays each window in a vertical pane.

Cascaded windows

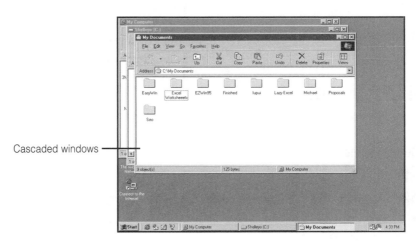

21

Cheat Sheet

Understanding Types of Icons

Disk icons	Used to represent the drives on your system. When you double-click a disk icon, you see the contents of that drive.
Folder icons	Used to represent the folders on your system (and they look like folders). When you double-click a folder icon, you see the contents of that folder.
Program icons	Used to represent the programs on your system. Double-click a program icon to start that program.
Document icons	Used to represent the documents on your system (and they look like little documents). Double-click a document icon to open that document and start the program associated with the document.
Shortcut icons	Used to represent other items, such as a folder or program.

Moving Icons

1. Click the icon you want to move.
2. Drag it to the location you want.

Arranging Icons

1. To arrange icons on the desktop, right-click a blank part of the desktop. To arrange icons in a window, right-click a blank part of the window.
2. Select the Arrange Icons command. From the submenu that appears, select the arrangement you want.

5

Working with Icons

In Windows, items are represented by icons (little pictures); you can display, move, and arrange icons as covered here.

Basic Survival

Understanding Types of Icons

When you use Windows, you can expect to see the following types of icons:

Disk icons	Disk icons	Used to represent the drives on your system. When you double-click a disk icon, you see the contents of that drive.
Folder icons	Folder icons	Used to represent the folders on your system (and they look like folders). When you double-click a folder icon, you see the contents of that folder.
Program icons	Program icons	Used to represent the programs on your system. Double-click a program icon to start that program.
Document icons	Document icons	Used to represent the documents on your system (and they look like little documents). Double-click a document icon to open that document and start the program associated with the document.

| | Shortcut icons | Used to represent other items, such as a folder or program. You can set up shortcut icons as covered in Chapter 11. |

Moving Icons

You can move an individual icon around on the desktop or within a window. To do so, follow these steps:

1. Click the icon you want to move.

2. Drag it to the location you want.

Beyond Survival

Arranging Icons

You can also have Windows arrange icons for you, again on the desktop or within a window. You can select from several arrangements (by name, type, size, date). To do so, follow these steps:

1. To arrange icons on the desktop, right-click a blank part of the desktop. To arrange icons in a window, right-click a blank part of the window.

2. Select the Arrange Icons command. From the submenu that appears, select the arrangement you want.

Select the icon arrangement

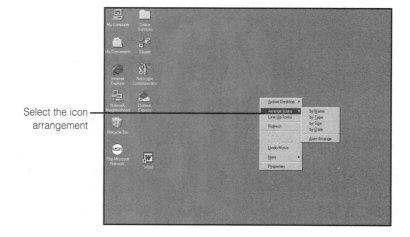

Lining Up Icons

If you want to align icons to an underlying grid (straighten them up), follow these steps:

1. To line up icons on the desktop, right-click a blank part of the desktop. To line up icons in a window, right-click a blank part of the window.

2. Select the Line Up Icons command. The icons are adjusted.

You can also change the appearance of desktop icons. See Chapter 33, "Changing How the Desktop Looks," for the steps to make this change.

Cheat Sheet

Using Help Contents

1. Click the Start button and select the Help command.
2. If necessary, click the Contents tab.
3. Click any of the book topics until you see the help page you want.
4. Click the help page.
5. When you are finished reading the help information, close the window by clicking the Close button.

Using the Help Index

1. Click the Start button and select the Help command.
2. Click the Index tab.
3. Type the first few letters of the topic for which you want help.
4. Double-click the topic you want.
5. When you finish reading this information, close the window by clicking the Close button.

Searching for a Help Topic

1. Click the Start button and select the Help command.
2. Click the Search tab.
3. In the first text box, type the word or words you want to find.
4. Click the List Topics button.
5. Double-click the topic you want.
6. When you finish reading this information, close the window by clicking the Close button.

Getting Help

You really can't be expected to remember each command and feature of Windows. You will find that you will remember the day-to-day stuff, the tasks you perform all the time. But for less-often-used tasks, you might need a little reminder. You can use online help for these tasks.

You can use online help to look up a topic in one of three ways: using the table of contents, using the index, or searching for a topic.

Basic Survival

Using Help Contents

Follow these steps to look up a topic in the table of contents:

1. Click the Start button and select the Help command. The Windows Help dialog box appears.

2. If necessary, click the Contents tab. Windows displays the Contents tab, which contains a list of topics, each represented by a book icon. You can open any of these topics.

3. Click any of the book topics. Windows displays additional subtopics. Do this until you see a help "page." Help pages are indicated with question-mark icons.

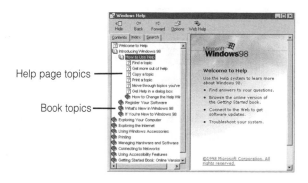

Help page topics

Book topics

4. Click the help page. The help information appears in the right part of the window.

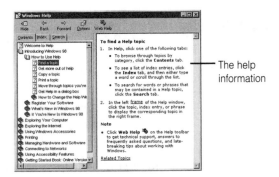

The help information

5. When you are finished reading the help information, close the window by clicking the Close button.

Using the Help Index

If you can't find the topic in the table of contents, you can also try looking up a topic using the index. Follow these steps:

1. Click the Start button and select the Help command.

2. Click the Index tab.

3. Type the first few letters of the topic for which you want help. Windows displays matching topics in the list box.

Windows displays matching topics in the list box.

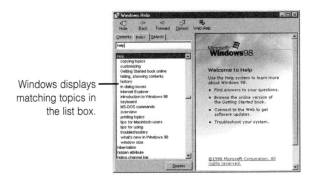

4. Double-click the topic you want. You see the appropriate help information.

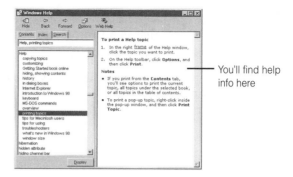

You'll find help info here

5. When you finish reading this information, close the window by clicking the Close button.

Beyond Survival

Searching for a Help Topic

If you can't find a topic by browsing the table of contents or looking it up in the index, you can search for a topic. Follow these steps:

1. Click the Start button and select the Help command.

2. Click the Search tab.

3. In the first text box, type the word or words you want to find.

4. Click the List Topics button. Windows displays matching topics in the list box.

If this is the first time you've used Search, the Find Setup Wizard appears. Click Next, then Finish. The wizard creates a word list for searching.

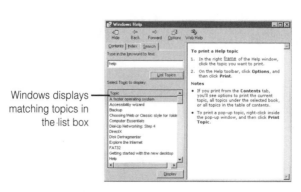

Windows displays matching topics in the list box

5. Double-click the topic you want. You see the help information for this topic.

6. When you finish reading this information, close the window by clicking the Close button.

PART
2

Working with Programs

You buy a computer so that you can use it to do things, and you do things using applications, or
programs. The best thing about Windows programs is that most programs operate in a similar fashion. After you learn a few key tasks, such as saving a document, you can use these skills in any Windows program. This part of the book covers the skills you can use in almost any type of application.(For information on using the programs included with Windows 98, see Part III, "Using Windows Accessories.") The following topics are covered:

- Working with Programs

- Starting a Program

- Switching Among Programs

- Installing and Uninstalling Programs

- Setting Up the Start Menu

- Creating Shortcuts

- Selecting Text

- Copying and Moving Text

- Saving a Document

- Opening a Document

- Closing a Document and Creating a New Document

- Printing a Document

Cheat Sheet

Starting a Program from the Start Menu

1. Click the Start menu and select Programs.
2. If necessary, open the program folder(s).
3. Click the icon to start the program.

Exiting a Program

1. Open the File menu and select the Exit command.

Starting a Program from a Shortcut Icon

1. Double-click the shortcut icon.

Starting a Program and Opening a Document

1. Click the Start button.
2. Select the Documents command.
3. Click the document you want to open.

Starting a Program with the Run Command

1. Click the Start button.
2. Select the Run command.
3. In the Open text box, type the program name, including the complete path to the program.
4. Click the OK button.

7

Starting a Program

The easiest way to start a program is by using the Start menu. After you get more proficient, you might want to investigate some shortcuts for starting programs.

Basic Survival

Starting a Program

The Start menu lists most of the programs you have on your system. These programs are organized into folders. To start a program, you open the folder that contains the program icon. Follow these steps:

1. Click the Start menu and select Programs. You see a list of the program folders and programs on your system.

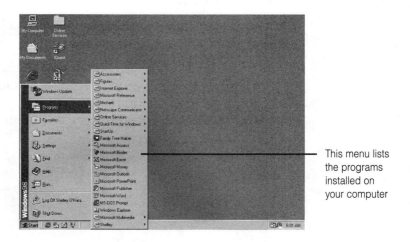

This menu lists the programs installed on your computer

2. If you see the program icon, click it to start the program.

If the program is stored in a folder, point to the folder. Do this until you see the program icon. Then click the icon to start the program.

Exiting a Program

When you are finished working in a program, save all your work. (See Chapter 14, "Saving a Document," for help on saving a document.) Then you can exit the program by following these steps:

1. Open the File menu.

2. Select the Exit command.

You can also click the Close (✕) button for the program window.

Beyond Survival

Starting a Program and Opening a Document

If you want to both open a document and start a program, you can use the Documents command. Windows keeps track of the last 15 documents you worked on. You can open any of these documents (and at the same time start that program) by following these steps:

1. Click the Start button.

2. Select the Documents command. You see a list of documents you have recently worked on.

3. Click the document you want to open. Windows starts the program and opens the document you selected.

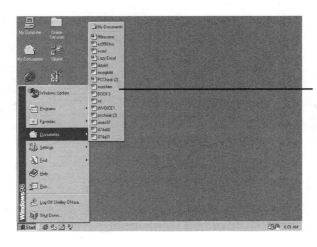

Select the Documents command to see a list of the last 15 documents you worked on

To clear the Documents menu, click Start, select Settings, and then click Taskbar & Start Menu. Click the Start Menu Programs tab, and then click the Clear button. Click OK.

Starting a Program with a Shortcut Icon

For programs you use all the time, you might want to put a shortcut to that program right on the desktop. Then you can simply double-click the shortcut icon to start the program.

Follow these steps to create a shortcut icon:

1. In Windows Explorer or My Computer, select the program for which you want to create a shortcut. Be sure that you can see at least part of the desktop. (For more help on displaying files, see Part IV, "Managing Files.")

2. With the right mouse button, drag the icon from the window to the desktop.

3. From the shortcut menu, select Create Shortcut(s) Here. Windows adds the shortcut to the desktop.

The shortcut is not the actual file, but a pointer to it. You can delete the shortcut by right-clicking it and selecting Delete. The original program, file, or folder is not affected.

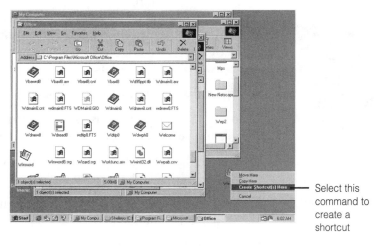

Select this command to create a shortcut

If you work in Web view in your desktop, you can single-click a program icon to start the program. For more information on Web view, see Chapter 35, "Viewing Your Desktop as a Web Page."

Starting a Program with a Shortcut Icon

You can also use the Run command to start a program. To use this command, you need to know the name of the program, as well as the path of folders where this program is stored. Usually Run is used to install new programs (refer to Chapter 7, "Starting a Program"). Follow these steps to use the Run command:

1. Click the Start button.

2. Select the Run command. You see the Run dialog box.

Type the name of the program you want to run

3. In the Open text box, type the program name. Be sure to include the complete path to the program. If you aren't sure where the program is stored, you can use the Browse button to browse through the folders on your system, finding the file you want.

4. Click the OK button. The program is started.

Starting a Program Each Time You Start Windows

As a final method, you can also put programs in your Startup folder. Each time you start Windows, all programs in this folder are started. Follow these steps:

1. Right-click on the Start button and select Explore.

2. In the pane on the left, display the program icon for the program you want to add to your Startup folder.

3. In the right pane, double-click the Programs folder and then double-click the StartUp folder.

4. Drag the program file from the pane on the left to the StartUp folder on the right.

5. Click the Close button.

Each time you start Windows, this program will be started.

To remove a program from the StartUp folder, right-click the Start button and select Explore. Then double-click the Programs folder and double-click the StartUp folder. Right-click on the icon you want to delete and select the Delete command.

Cheat Sheet

Switching Among Open Programs

1. Click the taskbar button for the program you want.

Switching Among Open Programs Using the Keyboard

1. Press Alt+Tab until you highlight the program you want.

Minimizing All Programs (and Windows)

1. Right-click a blank part of the taskbar.

2. Select Minimize All Windows.

8

Switching Among Programs

Another useful thing about Windows is its capability to run more than one program at a time. You can switch from program to program. For instance, if you are typing a report in a word processing program, you can switch to your spreadsheet program to review (and even copy data from) sales data.

Basic Survival

Switching Among Programs

Windows displays a button in the taskbar for each window that is open and program that is running. The button for the current program (or window) appears pressed. To switch to a different program, click the taskbar button for that program.

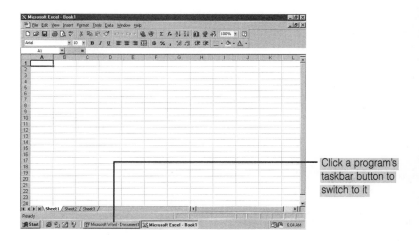

Click a program's taskbar button to switch to it

Beyond Survival

Using the Keyboard to Switch

If you used Windows 3.1, you might have gotten used to switching programs using the Alt+Tab key combination. You can also switch to a different program in Windows 95 or 98 by using the same key combination. Follow these steps:

1. Press Alt+Tab. You see a little toolbar with icons for each program that is running.

2. Press Alt+Tab until the program you want is boxed. When you release the keys, Windows switches to that program.

Minimizing All Programs (and Windows)

If you want to minimize all programs and open windows (close the windows onscreen but leave them running), follow these steps:

1. Right-click a blank area of the taskbar.

2. Select Minimize All Windows. All open windows and programs are minimized to a button on the taskbar.

Cheat Sheet

Installing a New Program

1. Insert the installation disk in the drive.
2. Click the Start button, select Settings, and then select Control Panel.
3. Double-click the Add/Remove Programs icon.
4. If necessary, click the Install/Uninstall tab.
5. Click the Install button.
6. When Windows finds the installation file on the disk, click the Finish button to run this program.
7. Follow the onscreen instructions for installing that particular program.

Uninstalling a Program

1. Click the Start button, select Settings, and then select Control Panel.
2. Double-click the Add/Remove Programs icon.
3. If necessary, click the Install/Uninstall tab.
4. Select the program you want to uninstall.
5. Click the Add/Remove button.

Adding Windows Components

1. Click the Start button, select Settings, and then select Control Panel.
2. Double-click the Add/Remove Programs icon.
3. Click the Windows Setup tab.
4. Check the components you want to install.
5. Click the OK button.
6. When prompted, insert the Windows disks or CD-ROM disc.

9

Installing and Uninstalling New Programs

When you purchase a new PC, that system might come with some software programs. These programs should be enough to get you started, but as you use the PC more and more, you might find that you require other programs. You might want to upgrade an existing program to the newest version, or you might want to purchase an entirely new program.

If you no longer you use a program, you can uninstall it. Finally, when Windows is installed, some components might not have been set up. You can check and add other Windows components.

Basic Survival

Purchasing a New Program

You can find software in some retail stores, in computer stores, and through mail-order outlets. Scan through any computer magazine to get an idea of what programs are available, as well as the cost. You can also use the Internet as a resource for researching and finding programs. You can even find freeware and shareware at many Internet sites. Freeware programs are provided free to you. Shareware programs are provided to you to try without cost. If you like the program, you can pay a small fee to register and continue using the program.

When you are looking for a new program to purchase, be sure that you can run that program on your system. Each program has system requirements—the type of microprocessor, amount of memory, hard-disk space, video card, and any other required equipment. You can usually find these requirements printed on the side of the software box. Check the requirements to be sure that your PC is capable of running the software.

Also, be sure that you get the right program for your system. If you have Windows 98, get Windows 98 programs. You can also purchase and run DOS and Windows 3.1 programs on Windows 95 and 98. If you have a Macintosh, get Macintosh programs. Most popular programs come in several versions.

As a final precaution, check to see how the software is distributed—on floppy disks or on a CD-ROM disc. If you have both a floppy disk and a CD-ROM drive, you don't have to worry. But if you don't have a CD-ROM drive, be sure to get the version on floppy disks. CD-ROM discs have become the most popular method for distributing programs, especially large programs.

Installing a New Program

When you install a new program, the installation program copies the necessary program files from the disk(s) to your hard disk and also sets up program icon(s) for the program. You need to specify which folder to use for the program files, where to place the program icons in the Start menu, and what program options you want to set. The options will vary depending on the program, but you don't have to worry too much because the installation program will guide you step-by-step through the process. You simply have to get the installation program started.

Windows provides an Add/Remove Programs icon you can use to install new programs and remove (or uninstall programs). Follow these steps:

1. Click the Start button, select Settings, and then select Control Panel. You see the program icons in the Control Panel.

2. Double-click the Add/Remove Programs icon.

3. If necessary, click the Install/Uninstall tab. You see the options for installing and uninstalling programs.

Use this tab to install or uninstall programs

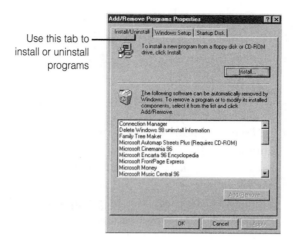

4. Click the Install button. You are prompted to insert the disk.

5. Insert the installation disk in the drive and click the Next button. If you are installing from a CD-ROM disc, that disc might have an AutoRun feature. If so, when you insert the disc, the installation program starts automatically.

Windows looks on the floppy drive and CD-ROM disc for an installation program. It then displays the name of this program in the dialog box. If this isn't the correct file, you can type the path or use the Browse button to select the Installation program file.

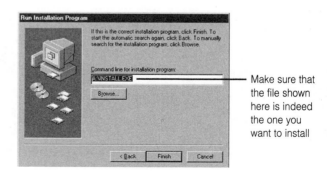

Make sure that the file shown here is indeed the one you want to install

6. Click the Finish button to run this program. Windows starts the program's installation program.

7. Follow the onscreen instructions for installing that particular program.

Uninstalling a Program

If you have a program you no longer need, or if you upgrade a program and want to get rid of the previous version, you can uninstall it. You could simply delete the program folder, but keep in mind that the original program installation might have put files in other folders and also changed some system settings. The best way is to uninstall a program using the Add/Remove Program icon. Follow these steps:

1. Click the Start button, select Settings, and then select Control Panel. You see the program icons in the Control Panel.

2. Double-click the Add/Remove Programs icon.

3. If necessary, click the Install/Uninstall tab. You see the options for installing and uninstalling programs.

4. Select the program you want to uninstall. If the program is not listed in this dialog box, you cannot use this method. Check the program documentation for information on uninstalling the program.

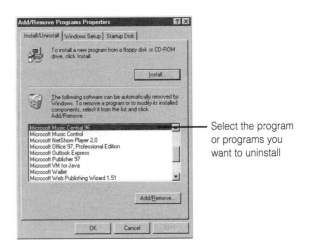

Select the program or programs you want to uninstall

5. Click the Add/Remove button. Windows removes the program files and any shortcuts to the program.

Beyond Survival

Using the Run Command to Install a Program

You can also install a program by using the Run command to run the installation program. To use this method, you need to know the exact name of the program. It's usually named something like INSTALL.EXE or SETUP.EXE. Follow these steps to use the Run command:

1. Insert the program disk into the drive.

2. Click the Start button.

3. Select the Run command. The Run dialog box appears.

4. In the Open text box, type the program name. Remember to type the drive letter. Your floppy drive is usually drive A. Your CD-ROM disc is usually drive D.

If you aren't sure of the name of the installation program, type the drive name and then use the Browse button to browse through the files on that drive. Select the installation file.

Remember to type your drive letter when entering the name of the program you want to install

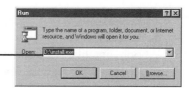

5. Click the OK button.

6. Follow the onscreen instructions for installing the program.

Adding Windows Components

When you install Windows, you have some options regarding which program components are installed. If you did not install Windows—or if you did and want to add other components (games, wallpaper, other program features)—you can do so using the Add/Remove Programs icon. Follow these steps:

47

1. Click the Start button, select Settings, and then select Control Panel. You see the program icons in the Control Panel.

2. Double-click the Add/Remove Programs icon.

3. Click the Windows Setup tab. You see the Windows components. Items in the Components list that are checked are installed. Items that are blank are not installed. If there's a gray background and a check, only some of the items in that set are installed.

Checked items in the components list are installed. Unchecked items are not installed. A gray background indicates that only some items in the set are installed

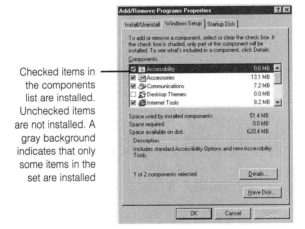

4. Check the components you want to install. Some components, like Accessories, consist of more than one program. To view the available options, select the component and then click the Details button. Check which components you want to install, and then click the OK button.

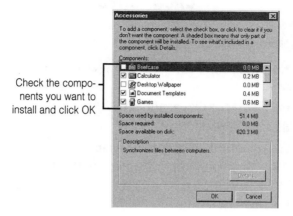

Check the compo-
nents you want to
install and click OK

5. Click the OK button.

6. When prompted, insert the Windows disks or CD-ROM disc. The necessary program files are copied to your Windows folder, and this component is added.

Cheat Sheet

Adding Programs to the Start Menu

1. Open the Start menu, select the Settings command, and select Taskbar & Start Menu.
2. Click the Start Menu Programs tab.
3. Click the Add button.
4. Enter the command line for the program you want to add. Or click the Browse button and select the program by browsing through the folders on your system.
5. Click the Next button.
6. Select the folder in which you want to place the program, and click the Next button.
7. Enter a name in the text box or accept the one Windows displays. Click the Finish button to add the new program.

Deleting Programs on the Start Menu

1. Open the Start menu, select the Settings command, and select Taskbar & Start Menu.
2. Click the Start Menu Programs tab.
3. Click the Remove button.
4. Display the program you want to remove. To do so, you might need to expand the folder listings. Click the plus sign next to the folder that contains your program.
5. Select the program you want to remove.
6. Click the Remove button.
7. Click the Close button to close this dialog box.
8. Click the OK button to close the Taskbar Properties dialog box.

Setting Up the Start Menu

You can control which items appear on the Start menu. For example, you can add programs, delete programs, add folders, and change where items are placed. You can set up the Start menu so that it is organized the way you want it.

Basic Survival

When you install a new program, the installation program usually takes care of adding the program to the Start menu. If it isn't added, you can add it yourself. Follow these steps:

1. Open the Start menu, select the Settings command, and select Taskbar & Start Menu. You see the Taskbar Properties dialog box.

2. Click the Start Menu Programs tab.

3. Click the Add button. You see the Create Shortcut dialog box.

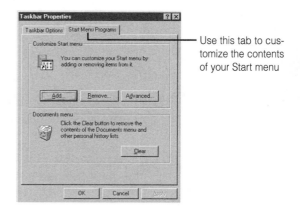

Use this tab to customize the contents of your Start menu

4. Enter the command line for the program you want to add. Alternatively, click the Browse button and select the program by browsing through the folders on your system.

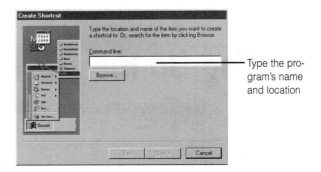

Type the program's name and location

5. Click the Next button. You are prompted to select a folder for the new program.

6. Select the folder in which you want to place the program, and click the Next button.

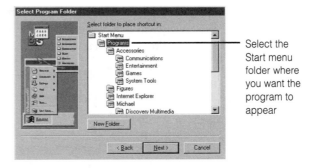

Select the Start menu folder where you want the program to appear

To create a new folder, click the New Folder button. Type the name and press Enter.

7. Enter a name in the text box or accept the one Windows displays. Click the Finish button to add the new program.

Enter a descriptive shortcut name here if you don't like the name Windows provides

Deleting Programs on the Start Menu

If your Start menu becomes cluttered, you might want to delete icons for programs you don't use. At first, you might go a little crazy and add all kinds of icons. Then after you use the computer more and more, you might want to streamline the Start menu and weed out programs that are not used.

Keep in mind that removing a program from the Start menu does not remove the program and its files from your hard disk. To do this, you can uninstall the program or manually delete the program and its related folders and files. See Chapter 29, "Deleting and Undeleting Files."

To remove an item from the Start menu, follow these steps:

1. Open the Start menu, select the Settings command, and select Taskbar & Start Menu. You see the Taskbar Properties dialog box.

2. Click the Start Menu Programs tab.

3. Click the Remove button. You see the Remove Shortcuts/Folder dialog box.

4. Display the program you want to remove. To do so, you might need to expand the folder listings. Click the plus sign next to the folder that contains your program.

5. Select the program you want to remove.

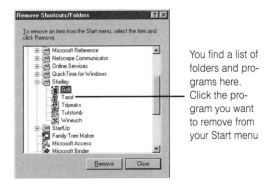

You find a list of folders and programs here. Click the program you want to remove from your Start menu

6. Click the Remove button.

7. Click the Close button to close this dialog box.

8. Click the OK button to close the Taskbar Properties dialog box.

Beyond Survival

Adding Folders to the Start Menu

If your Start menu becomes really huge, you might want to organize the programs into folders. Some programs set up folders for themselves; in addition, Windows sets up some folders on its own. You can also add new folders yourself and then move the program icons to the new folder. For instance, you might set up folders by task or program, or for each person who uses the PC.

Follow these steps to add a folder:

1. Open the Start menu, select the Settings command, and select Taskbar & Start Menu. You see the Taskbar Properties dialog box.

2. Click the Start Menu Programs tab.

3. Click the Advanced button. You see the Start menu in Windows Explorer.

4. Select the folder in which the new folder should be placed. You might need to expand the list to see the folder.

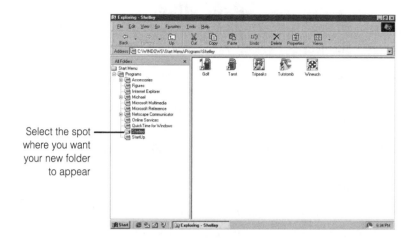

Select the spot where you want your new folder to appear

5. Open the File menu, select the New command, and then select Folder.

6. Type a name for the folder and press Enter. The folder is added.

7. Click the Close (×) button.

8. Click the OK button.

Rearranging the Start Menu

After you set up folders, you can organize your Start menu, putting the program icons in the folder and order you want. Rearranging the Start menu is similar to moving or copying files or folders (covered in Part IV). Follow these steps:

1. Open the Start menu, select the Settings command, and select Taskbar & Start Menu. You see the Taskbar Properties dialog box.

2. Click the Start Menu Programs tab.

3. Click the Advanced button. You see the Start menu in Windows Explorer.

4. Click the icon or folder, and then drag it to the folder where you want it placed. Do this for each program you want to move.

5. Click the Close (×) button.

6. Click the OK button.

Cheat Sheet

Creating a Shortcut

1. In Windows Explorer or My Computer, select the program, file, or folder for which you want to create a shortcut.
2. With the right mouse button, drag the icon from the window to the desktop.
3. From the shortcut menu, select Create Shortcut(s) Here.

Using a Shortcut

- Double-click a folder shortcut to see the contents of that folder.
- Double-click a file shortcut to open that file.
- Double-click a program shortcut to start the program.

Renaming a Shortcut Icon

1. Right-click the icon.
2. Select the Rename command.
3. Type a new name and press Enter.

Deleting a Shortcut Icon

1. Right-click the icon.
2. Select the Delete command.

11

Creating Shortcuts

In your work, you might find that there's one program, folder, or file you use all the time. You can create a shortcut to that program, file, or folder and place the shortcut on the desktop. You can then use this shortcut icon for quick access to the item.

Basic Survival

Creating a Shortcut

The hardest part about creating an icon is finding the actual file, program, or folder you want to create the shortcut to. After it is displayed, creating the shortcut is simply a matter of dragging and dropping it to the desktop. If you need help with finding or displaying files, see Part IV, which covers these tasks.

Follow these steps to create a shortcut:

1. In Windows Explorer or My Computer, select the program, file, or folder for which you want to create a shortcut. Be sure that you can see at least part of the desktop.

2. With the right mouse button, drag the icon from the window to the desktop.

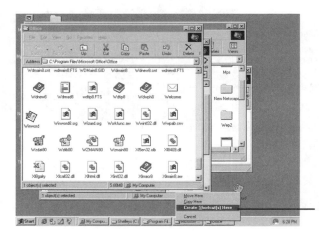

Right-drag the icon from the window to the desktop to begin creating a shortcut icon

3. From the shortcut menu, select Create Shortcut(s) Here. Windows adds the shortcut to the desktop.

Deleting a Shortcut Icon

After the shortcut is added, you simply double-click to access the icon. If you double-click a folder shortcut, you see the contents of that folder. When you double-click a file shortcut, that file is opened. Double-click a program shortcut to start the program.

Beyond Survival

Renaming a Shortcut Icon

When you create a shortcut icon, Windows names the icon Shortcut to *xxx*, where *xxx* is the filename. You might prefer a different name. You can easily rename a shortcut icon by following these steps:

1. Right-click the icon.

2. Select the Rename command. The current name is selected so that you can type a new name or edit the existing name.

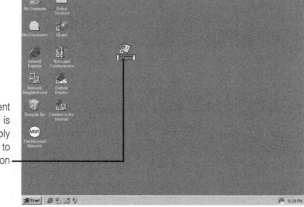

After the current name is selected, simply type over it to rename the icon

3. Type a new name and press Enter.

The shortcut is not the actual file, but a pointer to it. You can delete the shortcut icon if you don't need it. Sometimes, your desktop might become cluttered with all kinds of icons. If you don't use them, delete them so that your desktop is neat and tidy. Follow these steps to delete a shortcut icon:

1. Right-click the icon.

2. Select the Delete command.

The icon is removed from the desktop. The original program, file, or folder is not affected. If you want to delete the program from your hard disk, uninstall it as covered in Chapter 9, "Installing and Uninstalling New Programs."

Cheat Sheet

Selecting Text with the Mouse

1. Click at the start of the text you want to select.
2. Hold down the mouse button and drag across the text.
3. Release the mouse button. The text appears in reverse video.

Selecting Text with the Keyboard

1. Hold down the Shift key.
2. Use the arrow keys to highlight the text you want to select.

Selecting a Range in a Worksheet

1. Click the first cell you want to select.
2. Hold down the mouse button and drag across the other cells you want to select.
3. Release the mouse button.

Selecting an Object

1. Click the object.

12

Selecting Text

Although this book can't tell you how to use each of the applications you have on your PC, it can teach you some key skills used in many programs. Probably the most common skill is selecting something (text, numbers, an object). When you want to work with something, you start by selecting it. If you want to make text bold, you first select the text. If you want to chart a set of figures, you select the data to chart. If you want to copy an object you've drawn, you select that object. Selecting is the first step for many editing and formatting tasks.

Basic Survival

Selecting Text

To select text, follow these steps:

1. Click at the start of the text you want to select.

2. Hold down the mouse button and drag across the text.

3. Release the mouse button. The text appears in reverse video.

Selected text appears in reverse video —

After the text is selected, you can perform the editing or formatting task.

Beyond Survival

Selecting Text with the Keyboard

If you prefer to keep your hands on the keyboard, you can use it to select text. Follow these steps:

1. Hold down the Shift key.

2. Use the arrow keys to highlight the text you want to select.

Selecting a Range in a Worksheet

In a spreadsheet program, you follow a similar procedure for selecting a set of cells (called a *range*). For instance, you might want to select a set of cells to total. Follow these steps:

1. Click the first cell you want to select.

To select a graphics image, click it once.

2. Hold down the mouse button and drag across the other cells you want to select.

3. Release the mouse button.

Cheat Sheet

Deleting Text

1. Select the text you want to delete.

2. Press the Delete key.

Moving Text

1. Select the item you want to move. To select text or a range in a worksheet, drag across it. To select a graphics object, click it.

2. Click the Cut button, or open the Edit menu and select the Cut command.

3. Move the mouse to where you want to paste the text. Click once so that the cursor is in the correct place.

4. Click the Paste button, or open the Edit and select the Paste command.

Copying Text

1. Select the item you want to copy.

2. Click the Copy button, or open the Edit menu and select the Copy command.

3. Move the mouse to where you want to place the copy. Click once so that the cursor is in the correct place.

4. Click the Paste button, or open the Edit menu and select the Paste command.

13

Copying and Moving Text

One of the greatest benefits of an electronic document is that the data is not yet committed to paper; therefore, you can easily make editing changes. You can delete text you don't need, move text to a different location, or copy text you want to reuse.

If your program includes a toolbar, look for buttons for cutting, copying, and pasting.

Windows programs use the metaphor of scissors and paste for these editing tasks. You first "cut" the text you want to move or copy and then "paste" the text to its new location. You can find these commands in the Edit menu of most programs. The process for moving and copying text is similar from program to program.

Basic Survival

Deleting Text

To delete text, follow these steps:

1. Select the text you want to delete.

2. Press the Delete key. The other text is adjusted to fill in the gap.

Moving Text

To move text, follow these steps:

1. Select the item you want to move. To select text or a range in a worksheet, drag across it. To select a graphics object, click it.

Select the text you want to move

2. Click the Cut button, or open the Edit menu and select the Cut command.

3. Move the mouse to where you want to paste the text. Click once so that the cursor is in the correct place.

4. Click the Paste button, or open the Edit menu and select the Paste command. The text is pasted to the new location.

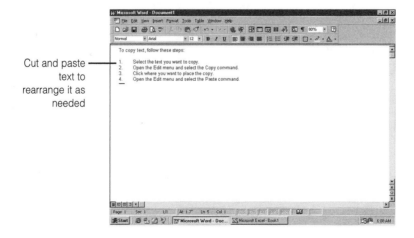

Cut and paste text to rearrange it as needed

Copying Text

Copying text is similar to moving text, but you will have two copies of the selected text: one in the original spot and one where you paste the copy. Follow these steps:

1. Select the item you want to copy.

2. Click the Copy button, or open the Edit menu and select the Copy command.

Select the text you want to copy

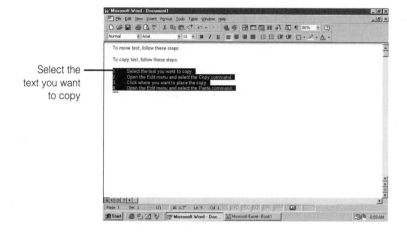

3. Move the mouse to where you want to place the copy. Click once so that the cursor is in the correct place.

4. Click the Paste button, or open the Edit menu and select the Paste command.

Paste the text

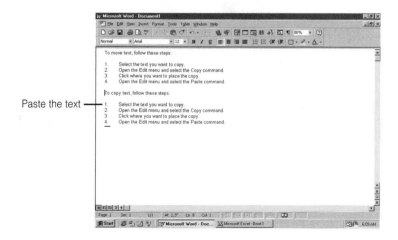

The text is pasted to the new location. You now have two copies of the selected text.

Beyond Survival

Copying to Another Program

You can also copy data from one program to another. If you simply copy and paste, the data is pasted in the receiving program in an acceptable format. For instance, if you copy Excel data to a Word document, it is pasted as a table. You can also insert the data as an object (like a mini-document from the program). You can then edit the inserted object using the original program.

Follow these steps to copy data to another program:

1. Select the item you want to copy.

2. Click the Copy button, or open the Edit menu and select the Copy command.

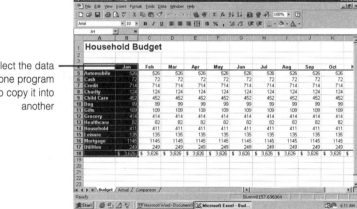

Select the data in one program to copy it into another

3. Switch to the program into which you want to paste the data. (Remember: To switch programs, use the taskbar buttons.)

4. Click in the document in the location where you want to paste the data.

68

5. To simply paste the data, click the Paste button, or open the Edit menu and select the Paste command.

To paste the data as an object, open the Edit menu and select the Paste Special command. Select the format for the data and click OK.

You can paste the data as an object, meaning that you decide how that data will appear in the new document

The data is pasted to the new program (here as an Excel object).

Note how this data, pasted into a Word document as an Excel object, retains some characteristics of a spreadsheet

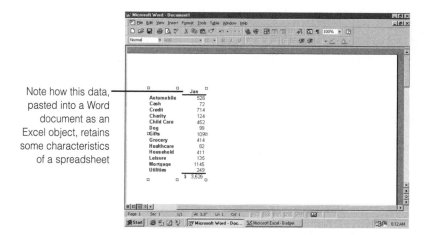

Cheat Sheet

Saving a Document the First Time

1. Open the File menu and select the Save command.
2. Select a drive from the Save in drop-down list.
3. Select a folder from the folders listed. You can use the Up One Level button to move up one folder in the folder structure.
4. Type a filename.
5. Click the Save button.

Saving a Document Again

1. Open the File menu and select the Save command.

Saving a Document with Another Name

1. Open the File menu and select the Save As command.
2. To save the file on another drive, select a drive from the Save in drop-down list.
3. To save the file in another folder, select a folder from the folders listed. You can use the Up One Level button to move up one folder in the folder structure.
4. Type a new filename.
5. Click the Save button.

Saving a Document

One of the most important things you can learn about using a PC is to save your work. Nothing is more frustrating than spending hours getting every word in a document just perfect and then having some accident happen before you've saved. If the power goes off, if your system crashes, if you turn off the PC without saving—all that work is lost. You should get in the habit of saving your work and saving often.

Basic Survival

Saving a Document the First Time

When you save a document the first time, you do two things. First, you select a location for the file—a folder on your hard disk where the file will be stored. Second, you enter a name. You can enter up to 255 characters—including spaces—for a name if you are using Windows 95 or 98. (Previous versions of Windows limited you to an 8-character name.) Use something descriptive, but don't go overboard.

You can type up to 255 characters for a filename, including spaces.

Again, the procedure for saving a document is similar from application from application. The following steps use Word as an example. In your program, you might find other features and options for saving, but the general process is the same.

Follow these steps to save a document:

1. Open the File menu and select the Save command. You see the Save As dialog box.

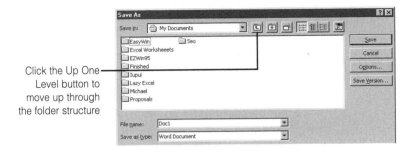

Click the Up One Level button to move up through the folder structure

Look for a Save button in the toolbar as a shortcut for selecting the Save command.

2. Select a drive from the Save in drop-down list.

3. Select a folder from the folders listed. You can use the Up One Level button to move up one folder in the folder structure.

4. Type a filename.

5. Click the Save button.

Saving a Document Again

After you've saved the document once, you don't have to reenter the folder name and filename. You can simply select File, Save to save the document to the same folder and with the same name.

Beyond Survival

Saving a Document with Another Name

You can change the name and folder for a document using the Save As command. You can also use this command to save a copy of a file. The original remains intact, and you also create a new file with the new name. Follow these steps:

1. Open the File menu and select the Save As command. You see the Save As dialog box. The original name and folder are listed.

2. To save the file on another drive, select a drive from the Save in drop-down list.

3. To save the file in another folder, select a folder from the folders listed. You can use the Up One Level button to move up one folder in the folder structure.

4. Type a new filename.

5. Click the Save button.

Saving a Document As Another File Type

Occasionally, you might need to share files with someone who does not use the same program as you. Most programs enable you to save a file in various formats. For instance, if you have Word for Windows (a word processing program), you can save a document as a Word file, a plain-text file, a formatted text file, and several other choices. Follow these steps to save a document as another file type:

1. Open the File menu and select the Save As command. You see the Save As dialog box. The original name and folder are listed.

2. To save the file on another drive, select a drive from the Save in drop-down list.

3. To save the file in another folder, select a folder from the folders listed. You can use the Up One Level button to move up one folder in the folder structure.

4. To save the file with a different name, type a new filename.

5. Display the Save as type drop-down list and select the appropriate file type.

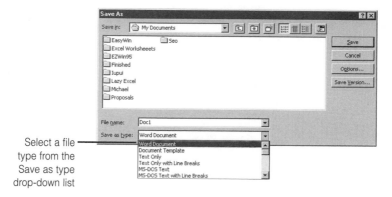

Select a file type from the Save as type drop-down list

6. Click the Save button. The document is saved in the new format.

73

Cheat Sheet

Opening a Document

1. Open the File menu and select the Open command.
2. If necessary, change to the drive and folder that contains the file. You can use the Look in drop-down list to select a different drive. Use the Up One Level button to move up a level in the folder structure.
3. When you see your file listed, double-click it.

Switching Among Open Documents

1. Open the Window menu.
2. Click the document you want.

Displaying All Open Documents

1. Open the Window menu.
2. Select the command for arranging windows.

15

Opening a Document

The purpose of saving a document is so that you can open it again. You might want to open a document and use it again. Or perhaps you weren't finished: you need to make additional editing or formatting changes. You can display the Open dialog box and then select the document you want to open.

Basic Survival

Opening a Document

When you want to work on a document you've saved previously, use the Open command. Follow these steps:

1. Open the File menu and select the Open command. You see the Open dialog box. The following figure shows the dialog box used for Word. The dialog box might look a little different for other programs.

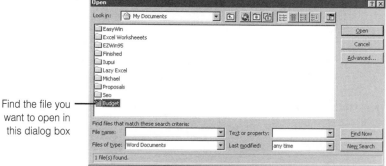

Find the file you want to open in this dialog box

As a shortcut, look for an Open button in the program toolbar.

2. If necessary, change to the drive and folder that contains the file. You can use the Look in drop-down list to select a different drive. Use the Up One Level button to move up a level in the folder structure.

3. When you see your file listed, double-click it.

Beyond Survival

Switching Among Open Documents

Just as you can have more than one program running, in most Windows programs you can work in more than one document. You might copy data, for instance, from one document to another. While writing, you might have open your outline in one document and the current chapter in another. To open another document, simply use File, Open.

To switch among open documents, follow these steps:

1. Open the Window menu. You see a list of all open documents. The current document is indicated with a check mark.

The Window menu lists documents that are currently open in that program

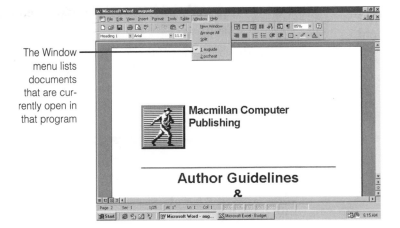

2. Click the document you want. That document becomes the active document.

Displaying All Open Documents

In addition to being able to switch among documents, many programs provide commands for arranging all open documents. The options will vary, but the basic process is the same. Follow these steps:

1. Open the Window menu. Look for a command named Arrange, Arrange All, or something similar.

2. Select the command for arranging windows.

Cheat Sheet

Closing a Document

- Open the File menu and select the Close command.
- Click the Close (×) button for the *document* window. Be sure that you click the button for the document window and not the program window.
- Press Ctrl+F4.

Creating a New Document

1. Open the File menu and select the New command.
2. If you see a dialog box listing templates, select the one you want.
3. Click the OK button.

16

Closing a Document and Creating a New Document

When you are done working on a document, you can close it. When all documents are closed, you can either exit the program or create a new document. (For information on closing a program, see Chapter 7, "Starting a Program.") Creating a new document is also covered here.

Basic Survival

Closing a Document

After you save a document, the document remains open onscreen. When you are finished with the document, you can close it (and save resources). Do any of the following:

- Open the File menu and select the Close command.

- Click the Close (✕) button for the *document* window. Be sure that you click the button for the document window and not the program window.

- Press Ctrl+F4.

Creating a New Document

When you start most programs, you see a blank document onscreen. You can start typing away. What do you do when you want a new "sheet of paper"? Create a new document:

1. Open the File menu and select the New command. You might be prompted to select a template for the new document.

2. If you see a dialog box listing templates, select the one you want and click the OK button.

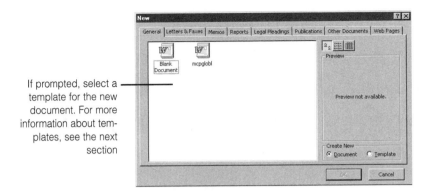

If prompted, select a template for the new document. For more information about templates, see the next section

Beyond Survival

Using a Template

A template is a predefined document that can contain text and formatting. For instance, a memo template includes all the headings for a memo (To, From, and so on). Depending on the program, you might find different templates available for your use.

Cheat Sheet

Printing a Document

1. Open the File menu and select the Print command.
2. Make any changes to the print options.
3. Click the OK button.

Previewing a Document

1. Open the File menu and select the Print Preview command.

Setting Up a Document

1. Open the File menu and select the Page Setup command.
2. Make your selections.
3. Click the OK button.

Printing a Document

Most documents are created with the intent of being printed and possibly distributed. If your printer is connected, printing is as easy as selecting a command. If your printer is not set up, refer to Chapter 47, "Setting Up Your Printer."

Basic Survival

Printing a Document

You can print in most programs using the File, Print command. What might be different are the options you can select for printing. You might be able to select the printer to use, the number of copies to print, what to print, and more. You make these selections in the Print dialog box. Follow these steps to print a document:

1. Open the File menu and select the Print command. Most programs display a Print dialog box, where you can select such printing options as what to print and the number of copies to print.

Look for a Print button as a shortcut for printing. Or use the keyboard shortcut: Ctrl+P.

Select printing options here

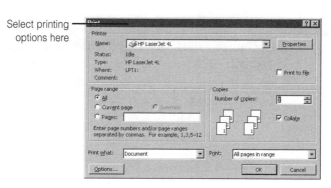

2. Make any changes to the options.
3. Click the OK button.

Beyond Survival

Previewing a Document

Most programs enable you to preview a document before printing. Doing so lets you get a sense of how the document will print on the page. You can then make any changes (like adjust the margins) *before* you print.

To preview a document, look for a Print Preview command in the File menu. The following figure shows a preview of a document in Word.

Use Print Preview to get a sense of how your document will look on paper *before* you print

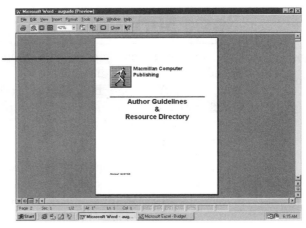

Setting Up a Document Page

Want to change the margins? Add a header or footer? Most programs provide formatting features for changing the look of the page. For content changes, look in the Format menu. For page changes, try the File, Page Setup command. The following figure shows some of the available options for setting up a page in Word for Windows.

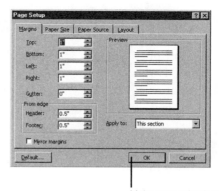

Make your selections in the
dialog box, and then click
the OK button

PART 3

Using Windows Accessories

To get you started, Windows includes some miniapplications or accessories. Some of these tools are basic programs you can use if your needs are simple. For instance, if you want a simple word processing program, try WordPad. Some are handy, like Calculator. Others are just fun: think Solitaire. This section covers how to work with the applications included in Windows. The following topics are covered:

- Using Windows Accessories
- Creating Documents with WordPad
- Creating Pictures with Paint
- Playing Sounds and Movies
- Sending and Receiving Faxes
- Playing Games
- Doing Calculations with Calculator
- Editing Text Files with Notepad

Cheat Sheet

Starting WordPad

1. Click the Start menu and select Programs.
2. Select the Accessories folder.
3. Click the WordPad program.

Typing and Editing Text

- To type text, simply start typing. You don't need to press Enter at the end of the line.
- Press Enter to end a paragraph and start a new one and to insert blank lines.
- You can use the arrow keys to move the insertion point, or you can point to the spot you want and click the mouse button.
- To delete text to the left of the insertion point, press Backspace. To delete text to the right of the insertion point, press Delete.
- To select text, hold down the mouse button and drag across the text you want to select.
- To delete a lot of text, select the text and then press Delete.
- To move text, select the text you want to move. Then open the Edit menu and select the Cut command. Move to where you want to place the text and select Edit, Paste.
- To copy text, select the text and then select Edit, Copy. Click where you want to place the text and then select Edit, Paste.
- Use the File, Save command to save your document.
- To print a document, use the File, Print command.

Formatting Text

1. Select the text you want to change.
2. Do any of the following:
   - To change the font, display the Font list and select the font you want to use.
   - To change the size of the text, display the Font Size list and then click the size you want.
   - To make text bold, click the Bold button.
   - To make text italic, click the Italic button.
   - To underline text, click the Underline button.
   - To change the color of text, click the Color button and then click the color you want to use.

Creating Documents with WordPad

Windows 98 includes a mini–word processing program named WordPad. If you need to create simple documents without a lot of fancy stuff, you can use WordPad. It includes the most basic editing and formatting features.

Basic Survival

Starting WordPad and Typing Text

You start WordPad as you do any Windows program:

1. Click the Start menu and select Programs.
2. Select the Accessories folder.
3. Click the WordPad program.

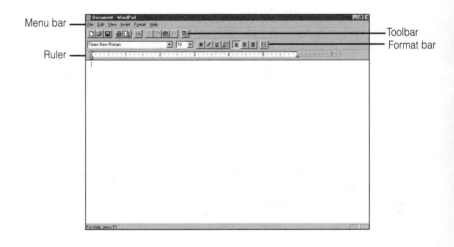

Menu bar, Ruler, Toolbar, Format bar

To type text, simply start typing. You don't need to press Enter at the end of the line. WordPad automatically wraps text to the next line. Press Enter to end a paragraph and start a new one and to insert blank lines.

Editing Text

To edit text, you move the insertion point to where you want to make a change. You can use the arrow keys to move the insertion point. Alternatively, point to the spot you want and click the mouse to place the insertion point.

After you have the insertion point in the right spot, you can do any of the following:

- To delete text to the left of the insertion point, press Backspace. To delete text to the right of the insertion point, press Delete.

- To select text, hold down the mouse button and drag across the text you want to select. Refer to Chapter 12, "Selecting Text," for more information on selecting text.

- To delete a lot of text, select the text and then press Delete.

- To move text, select the text you want to move. Then open the Edit menu and select the Cut command. Move to where you want to place the text and select Edit, Paste. Refer to Chapter 13, "Copying and Moving Text," for more information on moving and copying text.

- To copy text, select the text and then select Edit, Copy. Click where you want to place the text and then select Edit, Paste.

Remember to save!

- Remember to save your document! Chapter 14, "Saving a Document," covers saving a document.

- To print a document, use the File, Print command. You can find more help on printing in Chapter 17, "Printing a Document."

Formatting Text

You can use the buttons in the Format bar to change the appearance of text. Start by selecting the text you want to change. Then do any of the following:

- To change the font, display the Font list and select the font you want to use.

- To change the size of the text, display the Font Size list and then click the size you want.

- To make text bold, click the Bold button.

- To make text italic, click the Italic button.

- To underline text, click the Underline button.

- To change the color of text, click the Color button and then click the color you want to use.

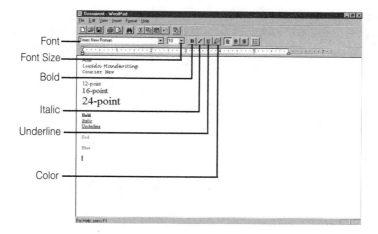

Beyond Survival

Formatting Paragraphs

You can also use the buttons in the Format bar to change the alignment of a paragraph. Click the Align Left, Center, or Align Right buttons.

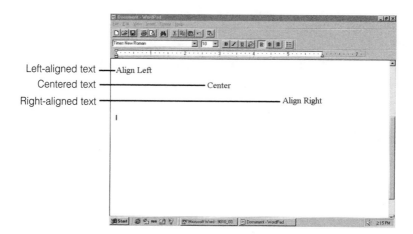

*Use Edit,
Undo to undo
a change.*

You can add bullets to a paragraph by selecting the paragraphs you want and then clicking the Bullets button.

You can also make changes using the Format, Paragraph command. In addition to changing the alignment, you can enter a value for a left indent, a right indent, or a first-line indent.

To set tabs for a paragraph, use the Format, Tabs command.

Formatting Pages

By default, the left and right margins of a WordPad document are 1.25 inches, and the top and bottom margins are 1 inch. You can make a change to the margins, paper size, and orientation by following these steps:

1. Open the File menu and select the Page Setup command. You see the Page Setup dialog box.

2. Click in the margin you want to change. Type the new value.

Type the —
new margin

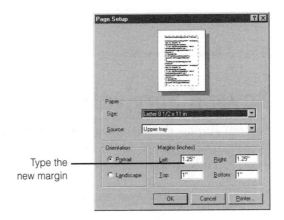

3. To select a different paper size, display the Size dropdown list and select the size.

4. To change the orientation, click the option button for Portrait or Landscape.

5. Click the OK button.$I~WordPad;pages;formatting>

Cheat Sheet

	Free-Form Select	Use to draw around the area you want to select. You can then copy or cut the area.
	Select	Use to select a part of the drawing. With this tool, you can draw a rectangular area for selection.
	Eraser/Color Eraser	Use to erase either part of the drawing or color from part of the drawing.
	Fill With Color	Use to fill a part of the drawing with color. Select the color from the color palette.
	Pick Color	Use to pick up a color to use in another part of the drawing.
	Magnifier	Use to zoom in on the drawing. Click the tool and then click the area you want to magnify.
	Pencil	Drag across the screen to "draw."
	Brush	Use to paint onscreen. You can select the size and shape of the paintbrush.
	Airbrush	Use to spray paint on the drawing. You can select the color and size of the splatter.
	Text	Use to draw a box for text.
	Line	Use to draw a line. You can select the thickness of the line.
	Curve	Use to draw a curved line. Click and drag to draw a straight line; then drag the line you drew to make the curve.
	Rectangle	Use to draw a rectangle. You can select to draw an empty or filled rectangle.
	Polygon	Use to draw a polygon (multisided object). Drag to draw the first side, release the mouse button, and drag to draw the next side. To complete the object, double-click.
	Ellipses	Use to draw a circle or an oval. You can draw one that is filled or empty. To draw a perfect circle, hold down the Shift key as you draw.
	Rounded Rectangle	Use to draw a rounded rectangle, filled or unfilled.

Creating Pictures with Paint

If you like to draw, you can create simple illustrations with Paint, another miniprogram included with Windows 98. You can draw simple shapes such as circles and squares. You can draw with the pencil or brush tools. And you can add color to the page. This chapter covers the basics of using Paint.

Basic Survival

Starting Paint

You start Paint as you do any Windows program:

1. Click the Start menu and select Programs.

2. Select the Accessories folder.

3. Click the Paint program.

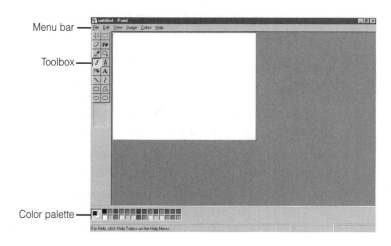

Menu bar

Toolbox

Color palette

Using the Toolbox

When you want to draw or edit an object, start by clicking the appropriate tool. The following table identifies each tool and explains how to draw or work with the tool.

	Free-Form Select	Use to draw around the area you want to select. You can then copy or cut the area.
	Select	Use to select a part of the drawing. With this tool, you can draw a rectangular area for selection.
	Eraser/Color Eraser	Use to erase either part of the drawing or color from part of the drawing.
	Fill With Color	Use to fill a part of the drawing with color. Select the color from the color palette.
	Pick Color	Use to pick up a color to use in another part of the drawing.
	Magnifier	Use to zoom in on the drawing. Click the tool and then click the area you want to magnify.
	Pencil	Drag across the screen to "draw."
	Brush	Use to paint onscreen. You can select the size and shape of the paintbrush.
	Airbrush	Use to spray paint on the drawing. You can select the color and size of the splatter.
	Text	Use to draw a box for text.
	Line	Use to draw a line. You can select the thickness of the line.
	Curve	Use to draw a curved line. Click and drag to draw a straight line; then drag the line you drew to make the curve.
	Rectangle	Use to draw a rectangle. You can select to draw an empty or filled rectangle.
	Polygon	Use to draw a polygon (multisided object). Drag to draw the first side, release the mouse button, and drag to draw the next side. To complete the object, double-click.
	Ellipses	Use to draw a circle or an oval. You can draw one that is filled or empty. To draw a perfect circle, hold down the Shift key as you draw.
	Rounded Rectangle	Use to draw a rounded rectangle, filled or unfilled.

Drawing an Object

You can use any of the drawing tools to draw onscreen. You can draw a line or a filled rectangle. You can use the simple shapes to compose a drawing. Follow these steps:

Remember to save your documents

1. Click the tool you want to use. You see the available options for that tool in the tool palette.

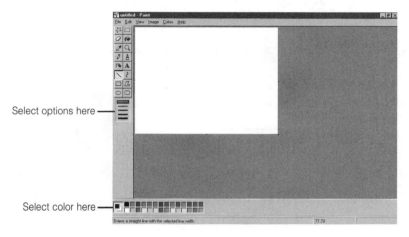

Select options here

Select color here

Right-click the color to use that color for the fill color.

2. To select an option, click it. For instance, for lines, you can select a thickness.

3. In the color box, click the color you want to use.

4. Click in the drawing area and drag to draw. The object is added to the drawing.

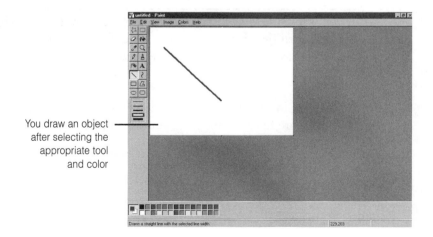

You draw an object after selecting the appropriate tool and color

Erasing Part of a Drawing

If you make a mistake, you can erase that part of the drawing using the Eraser/Color Eraser tool. Follow these steps:

1. Click the Eraser/Color Eraser tool.

2. Select the eraser size.

3. Drag across the part of the drawing you want to erase. That part is erased.

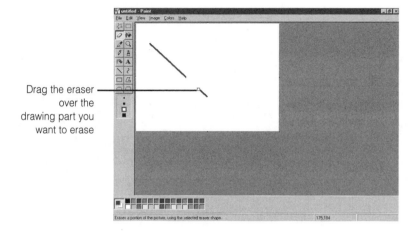

Drag the eraser over the drawing part you want to erase

To clear the entire drawing area, open the Image menu and select the Clear Image command.

Beyond Survival

If you want your drawing to include text, you can draw a text box and then type the text. You can select from different sizes and effects for the text. Follow these steps:

1. Click the Text tool.

2. Drag in the drawing area to draw the text box. When you are finished dragging, you see an insertion point inside the text box.

3. Type your text.

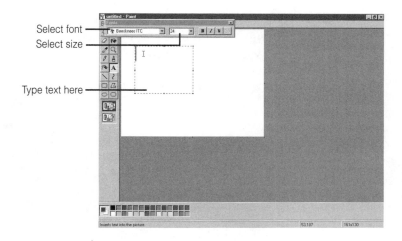

Select font

Select size

Type text here

4. Use the Fonts toolbar to make any changes to the text.

5. Click outside the text box to add the object to the drawing.

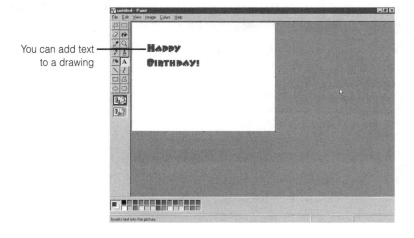

You can add text
to a drawing

HAPPY

BIRTHDAY!

Filling an Object with Color

You can fill in any bordered area with color. To do so, use the Fill With Color tool. Follow these steps:

1. Click the Fill With Color tool.

2. Click the color you want to use in the color palette.

Undo mis-
takes with
Edit, Undo

3. Move the tip of the pointer (which looks like a paint can about to spill) into the area to fill, and click. The area is filled with the selected color.

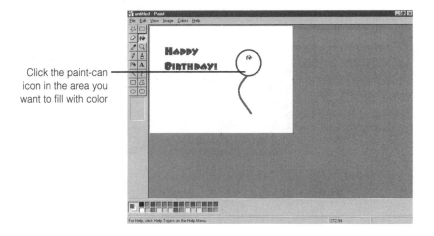

Click the paint-can
icon in the area you
want to fill with color

Copying an Object

If you get an object just perfect and want to use that same image again, you can copy it. Follow these steps:

1. Use the Free-Form Select or Select tools to draw around the object to copy.

2. Hold down the Ctrl key and drag a copy of the object to the location you want.

Cheat Sheet

Playing Music

1. Click the Start button, select Programs, select Accessories, select Entertainment, and select CD Player.
2. Insert a disc into your CD drive and click the Play button.

Playing Sounds

1. Click the Start button, select Programs, select Accessories, select Entertainment, and select Sound Recorder.
2. Open the File menu and select Open. In the Open dialog box that appears, change to the drive and folder that contains the sound file.
3. When you see the sound file you want to play, double-click it.
4. To play the sound, click the Play button.

Playing Media Clips and Movies

1. Click the Start button, select Programs, select Accessories, select Entertainment, and select Media Player.
2. Open the File menu and select Open.
3. Change to the drive and folder that contains the media file.
4. When you see the file you want to play, double-click it.
5. Click the Play button.
6. To close Media Player, click its Close (×) button.

20

Playing Sounds and Movies

Windows also includes several multimedia programs. You can play an audio CD, play sound files, and even record sounds. You can also play multimedia files.

Multimedia is the combination of different media—sound, video, text, graphics, animation, and so on. For example, you might have a multimedia encyclopedia. When you look up an entry for Beethoven, you cannot only read a text account of his life and accomplishments, but also play a sample of one of his symphonies. The entry might also include a picture of the famous composer.

To take advantage of these multimedia programs, you need a CD-ROM drive, a sound card, and speakers. As multimedia presentations and programs became more popular, the equipment to run these features became standard equipment on a PC. If you have a new PC, it probably has the necessary equipment. If you don't, you can purchase a multimedia upgrade package to add this equipment.

Basic Survival

Playing Music

If you like music, you can use CD Player (included with Windows 98) to play your audio CDs. Keep in mind that the sound quality isn't going to be as great as if you were playing the CDs on your CD player. Even though most sound cards come with speakers that are adequate for playing sounds, don't expect excellent quality.

To play a CD, follow these steps:

1. Click the Start button, select Programs, select Accessories, select Entertainment, and (finally) select CD Player. Windows starts the CD Player program.

2. Insert a disc into your CD drive and click the Play button. CD Player plays the first track on the CD. You can see the current track number and amount of time the CD has been playing in the CD Player window.

You can minimize the CD Player window, and the CD continues to play. Some systems have an AutoRun command that automatically starts the CD when you insert it into the drive.

Playing Sounds

Not only can you play audio CDs on your computer, but you also can play other sounds. For instance, a coworker might have recorded a message and attached it to a file. You can play the sound.

Sounds, like all information on a computer, are stored in files. Most sound files are WAV files. You can play back sounds you have recorded, or sounds provided with some other application. You also can download sounds from bulletin board systems or purchase sound files.

To play a sound, follow these steps:

1. Click the Start button, select Programs, select Accessories, select Entertainment, and select Sound Recorder. Windows displays the Sound Recorder window.

2. Open the File menu and select Open. In the Open dialog box that appears, change to the drive and folder that contains the file. Windows includes some sample sound files in the WINDOWS\MEDIA folder.

3. When you see the sound file you want to play, double-click it. In the Sound Recorder window, the name of the sound appears in the title bar.

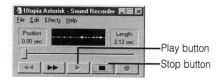

Play button
Stop button

4. To play the sound, click the Play button. Sound Recorder plays the sound. As it plays, you see the sound wave in the Sound Recorder window.

Playing Media Clips and Movies

If you have multimedia presentations, you can use the Windows Media Player to play them. (Windows includes some sample files in the WINDOWS\MEDIA folder.) You can play the following types of files:

• Video for Windows (AVI files)

• Sound (WAV files)

• MIDI music (MID and RMI files)

Many Internet sites also include movies you can play.

Follow these steps to play a media file:

1. Click the Start button, select Programs, select Accessories, select Entertainment, and select Media Player. Windows displays the Media Player program window.

2. Open the File menu and select Open. The Open dialog box appears with the Media folder selected. You can open files in this folder. Or if necessary, change to the appropriate drive and folder.

3. When you see the file you want to play, double-click it. You see the Media Player window with the name of the file in the title bar.

The Stop button

4. To play the media clip, click the Play button.

Beyond Survival

Playing a Different Track on a CD

You can select which track is played on the CD and also use the toolbar to control play. You can also enter the name of the artist, CD, and tracks.

To enter the name of the artist, CD, and tracks, follow these steps:

1. Open the Disc menu and select the Edit Play List command. You see the CD Player: Disc Settings dialog box.

Type name

Enter track name

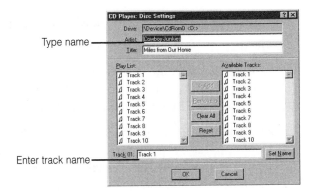

2. Type the name in the Artist text box.

3. Type the name of the CD in the Title text box.

4. To enter a track name, select the track in the Play List, type the track's name, and then click Set Name.

5. When you are done making changes, click the OK button.

To play a different track, follow these steps:

1. In the CD Player window, display the Track drop-down list.

2. Click the track you want to play.

The CD Player includes buttons that enable you to start a song over, switch to a different song, stop a song, and so on.

Name	Description
▸ Play	Starts playing the CD.
❚❚ Pause	Pauses the CD. To resume play, click the Play button again.
■ Stop	Stops the CD.
◄◄ Previous Track	Plays the previous track.
►► Next Track	Plays the next track.
►► Skip Forward	Moves forward within the current track.
◄◄ Skip Backward	Moves backward within the current track.
▲ Eject	Ejects the CD.

Recording Sounds

To record sounds, you need a sound card and a microphone, and the microphone must be plugged into your sound card. Most sound cards come with a microphone, but it might not have been connected. Check your sound-card manual for help on where to plug in the microphone.

Follow these steps to record a sound:

1. In the Sound Recorder window, open the File menu and select New.

2. Click the Record button to start recording.

3. Speak into the microphone to record your sound. You see a visual representation of the sound wave as you make your recording. Because sound files can be really huge, you should try to keep your message short and concise.

4. When you finish recording, click the Stop button. You can play back the sound by clicking the Play button.

5. To save the sound, open the File menu and select Save. The Save As dialog box appears.

6. In the Save As dialog box, change to the drive and folder where you want to store the file. Then type a filename in the File name text box and click the Save button.

Cheat Sheet

Sending a Fax

1. Click Start, Programs, Accessories, Fax, and then Compose New Fax to start.
2. Enter the name of the person and the fax number. Click Next.
3. Select the cover page you want to use and click Next. If you don't want a cover page, select No.
4. Type the subject and any notes you want to include with the fax.
5. If you selected to include a cover page, check Start note on cover page. Click Next.
6. Click Next to skip adding a file. Alternatively, click the Add File button and then select the file to attach.
7. Click Finish to send the fax.

Receiving and Viewing a Fax

1. Start Microsoft Exchange. Then double-click the Fax icon in the status bar.
2. If you have set up for automatic answer, any incoming faxes will be received. If you have set up for manual answer, click the Answer Now button. Microsoft Fax displays the status of the incoming fax and then places the fax in the Inbox of Microsoft Exchange.
3. Double-click the fax to view its contents.
4. To print the fax, click the Print button.
5. Click the Close button to exit Microsoft Fax.

21

Sending and Receiving Faxes

If you have a fax modem, you can send and receive faxes using Microsoft Fax, a program included with Windows. You can use this program to compose, send, and receive faxes from others.

Basic Survival

Sending a Fax

To use this program, you must first set up some information about your phone line and fax modem. To do so, set up Windows Messaging. Click Start, Programs, and then Windows Messaging. Then follow the steps in the wizard, making selections appropriate to your setup.

You can send a fax to anyone who has a fax line. You create the document using your PC and then fax it to another fax machine or another PC with a fax/modem. Windows includes a fax wizard that leads you step-by-step through the process of creating a fax.

Note that you cannot fax hard-copy versions of documents. You can fax only documents you have created electronically.

Follow these steps to compose and send a fax:

1. Click Start, Programs, Accessories, Fax, and then Compose New Fax to start.

2. Enter the name of the person and the fax number. Click Next. You can set up an address book of fax numbers and then select the recipient from the list. To view the address book, click the Address Book button.

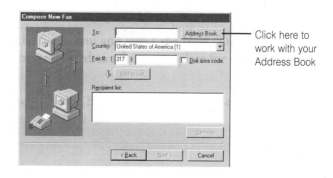

Click here to work with your Address Book

3. Select the cover page you want to use, and click Next. If you don't want a cover page, select No.

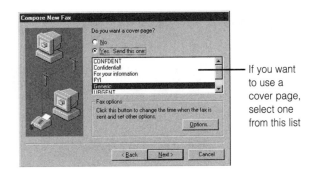

If you want to use a cover page, select one from this list

4. Type the subject and any notes you want to include with the fax.

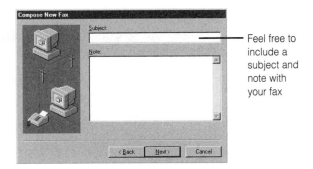

Feel free to include a subject and note with your fax

5. If you selected to include a cover page, check Start note on cover page. Click Next.

6. Click Next to skip adding a file. Alternatively, click the Add File button and then select the file to attach.

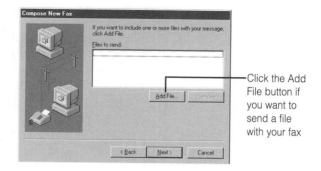

Click the Add
File button if
you want to
send a file
with your fax

7. Click Finish to send the fax.

**Receiving
and
Viewing a
Fax**

You can also use Microsoft Fax to receive faxes from others. You
can view them onscreen and print them. To receive a fax,
Microsoft Exchange must be running. You can set up Microsoft
Fax to answer automatically, or you can answer manually.
Follow these steps to receive and view a fax:

1. Start Microsoft Exchange. Then double-click the Fax
icon in the status bar.

2. If you have set up for automatic answer, any incoming
faxes will be received. If you have set up for manual
answer, click the Answer Now button. Microsoft Fax displays the status of the incoming fax and then places the
fax in the Inbox of Microsoft Exchange.

3. Double-click the fax to view its contents.

4. To print the fax, click the Print button.

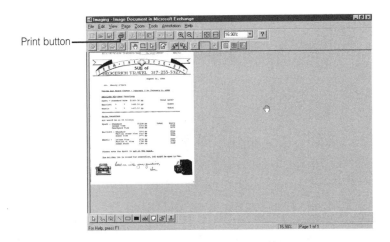

Print button

5. Click the Close button to exit Microsoft Fax.

Beyond Survival

**Dialing
Your Phone
with Phone
Dialer**

If your telephone is connected to your PC (or you have a built-in phone), you can dial numbers using Phone Dialer. Follow these steps:

1. Click Start, Programs, Accessories, Communication, and then Phone Dialer.

2. Type the number to dial. Or click the number buttons using the mouse. You can even set up Speed dial for numbers you frequently call.

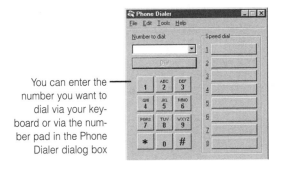

You can enter the number you want to dial via your keyboard or via the number pad in the Phone Dialer dialog box

3. Click the Dial button. When that person answers, pick up the phone receiver to talk.

Cheat Sheet

Playing Solitaire

The goal is to stack all the cards, aces to kings, in the upper-right piles. You have to stack them by suit.

Playing Hearts

When someone reaches 100 points, the game is over, and the person with the lowest score wins. Every trick you take with a heart is 1 point. The queen of spades is worth 13 points.

Playing FreeCell

The goal is to get all the cards stacked into four piles in the upper-right by suit, in order (aces to kings).

Playing Minesweeper

The goal is to clear all the mines.

22

Playing Games

Computers aren't all work. There's lots of fun to be had, and Windows includes some games you can play to relieve stress or boredom, including FreeCell, Hearts, Minesweeper, and Solitaire.

Basic Survival

Playing Solitaire

Probably the most popular (and easy to play) game is Solitaire. The computer version is just like the card version. To start the game, click Start, Programs, Accessories, Games, and then Solitaire.

If you don't see all of these games listed in your Games folder, they might not all have been installed. You can add them, as covered in Chapter 9, "Installing and Uninstalling New Programs."

The computer version of Solitaire is just like the card version

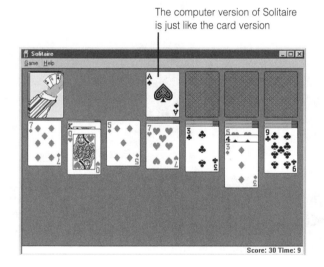

You can drag a card to another place. To turn over a card, click it. To start a new game, open the Game menu and select Deal.

Beyond Survival

**Playing
Hearts**

In addition to Solitaire, you can play Hearts. You play three other computer opponents. (If you are connected to an online service, like MSN, or to a network, you can also play with others who are online.) When someone gets to 100 points, the game is over (the object of the game is to have the lowest score at that time). Every trick you take with a heart is 1 point. The queen of spades is worth 13 points.

If you are daring, you can attempt to take all the hearts and the queen of spades. This is called "shooting the moon," and if you succeed, the other opponents each get 26 points.

You don't
want points
in Hearts.

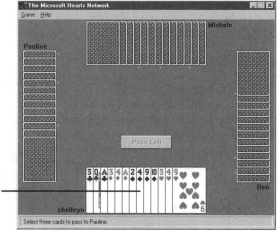

Shoot the moon by
taking all the hearts and
the queen of spades

**Playing
FreeCell**

FreeCell is another version of Solitaire. You try to get all the cards stacked into four piles in the upper-right by suit, in order (aces to kings). Use the four piles in the lower-right to move the cards around.

FreeCell is similar to Solitaire but can be a bit harder

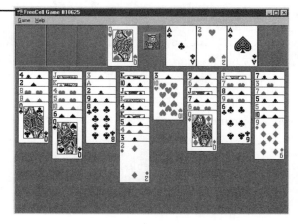

Playing Minesweeper

One game I've never had any success with is Minesweeper. To start, click on the board. You might lose instantly by hitting a mine; if you survive, keep clicking until you find places where you know mines exist. You must logically deduce where mines exist by looking at the numbers revealed under squares you've clicked; if a square has the numeral 1 on it, that numeral indicates that only one adjacent square has a mine under it. If only one adjacent square remains unclicked, you know that the mine is under that one square. Right-click that one square to designate it as a mine. If the square has a numeral 2 on it, two adjacent squares have mines under them, and so on. Continue in this manner until all the squares on the board are accounted for.

You know that a mine is under this square because all squares adjacent to the numeral 1 that is immediately above it are spoken for. Right-click it to mark it as a mine

119

Cheat Sheet

Figuring a Calculation

1. Click Start, Programs, Accessories, and then Calculator.

2. Type your equation, using the following operation keys:

+ add

- subtract

* multiply

/ divide

3. Press Enter to see the results.

Changing the Calculator

1. Open the View menu.

2. Select Scientific.

Using the Memory Functions

Click	To
MS	Store the value in memory
MR	Display the value stored in memory
MC	Clear the value in memory
M+	Add the value in memory

23

Doing Calculations with Calculator

Windows includes a little calculator, which is handy for performing quick calculations. You can use either the mouse or the keypad to input numbers.

Basic Survival

Figuring a Calculation

If you need a quick calculator, use the Windows online version. Follow these steps:

1. Click Start, Programs, Accessories, and then Calculator.

2. Click on the calculator to enter your equation. If you prefer, press the Num Lock key and use the numeric keypad for equations. You can use the following operators:

+ add

- subtract

* multiply

/ divide

3. To complete the equation and see the results, press Enter or click the equal (=) sign.

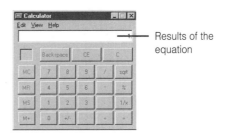

Results of the equation

Beyond Survival

Using the Clear and Memory Buttons

You can store a value in memory and then retrieve it using the Memory buttons. You can also clear entries.

Click	To
	Clear all values
	Clear only the current entry
	Delete the digit you just typed
	Store the value in memory
	Display the value stored in memory
	Clear the value in memory
	Add the value in memory

Changing the Calculator

If you need a more sophisticated calculator, change from the Standard to the Scientific. Open the View menu and select Scientific. This calculator gives you access to many more features and functions.

The Scientific calculator gives you access to many more features and functions than the Standard calculator

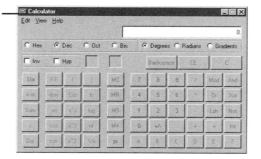

Cheat Sheet

Starting Notepad and Creating a Text File

1. Click Start, Programs, Accessories, and then Notepad.

2. Type the text you want to include.

3. Use File, Save to save the document.

Opening and Editing a Text File

1. Open the File menu and select the Open command.

2. Change to the folder and drive that contains the text file.

3. When you see the file listed, double-click it to open the file.

4. Make any editing changes.

5. Open the File menu and select the Save command to save the file.

Searching for Text in a Text File

1. Open the Search menu and select the Find command.

2. Type what you want to find.

3. Click the Find Next button.

24

Editing Text Files with Notepad

The most common type of file format is a simple text file. You can find program notes, installation guides, and configuration files saved as text files. If you need a way to view or edit this type of file, use Notepad. You might also want to create this type of file because almost any program can open a text file.

Basic Survival

Creating a Text File

To create a text file, start Notepad (click Start, Programs, Accessories, and then Notepad). Type the text. Keep in mind that Notepad does not automatically wrap lines. You must press Enter to insert line and paragraph breaks. (You can turn on word wrap by selecting the Edit, Word Wrap command.)

The main Notepad window —

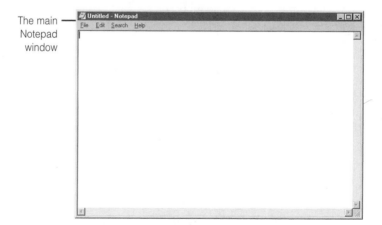

When you are done, you can open the File menu and select the Save command to save the document. Type a name and select a folder, and then click Save. (For more information on saving, see Chapter 14, "Saving a Document.)

When working in a text file, you can do the following:

- Insert the date in the text document with the Edit, Time/Date command.

Shortcut for inserting the date and time: F5.

- Open the Edit menu and select the Set Font command to select the font, font style, and size for the text. This font selection controls just the font used to display the file; the font is not saved when you save the file.

- Use the Edit, Copy command to copy text and the Edit, Cut command to cut text. Then paste the text using Edit, Paste.

- To print the document, use the File, Print command.

Opening and Editing a Text File

You can also open a text file to view its contents or to make a change. By default, Notepad displays all text files in the current folder. You can change to another drive or folder to open the file you want. Follow these steps:

1. Open the File menu and select the Open command.

2. Change to the folder and drive that contains the text file.

Change to a different drive

Move up one level

3. When you see the file listed, double-click it to open the file.

4. Make any editing changes.

5. Open the File menu and select the Save command to save the file.

Beyond Survival

Searching for Text in a Text File

In a short document, you can easily scan to find a word or phrase. In a longer document, scanning is not so easy. Instead, if you want to find a particular word or section in a text file, you can search for it. Follow these steps:

1. Open the Search menu and select the Find command.

Find a particular word or section in a text file by using the Find tool

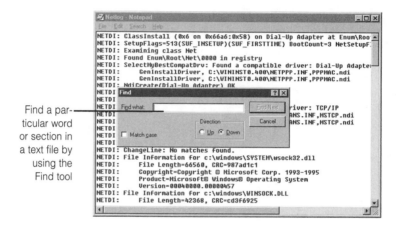

2. Type what you want to find.
3. Click the Find Next button. Notepad moves to the first match.

PART

4

Managing Files

After you start using a computer, you'll be surprised
how quickly the files pile up. You will have document
files, program files, and other types of files. To keep your
computer organized, you need to set up folders and store
similar files together. You should also periodically delete files
you don't need, and back up important files. This part of the
book covers all the key file-management tasks, including the
following:

- Managing Files

- Creating New Folders

- Selecting Files

- Moving and Copying Files

- Deleting and Undeleting Files

- Renaming Files or Folders

- Searching for Files

- Displaying Disk Properties

Cheat Sheet

Using My Computer to Display Files and Folders

1. Double-click the My Computer icon on your desktop.
2. Double-click the drive you want to open.
3. Double-click the folder you want to open.
4. Continue double-clicking folders until you find the folder or file you want to work with.
5. To close a window, click the Close button.

Changing the View

1. In the window, open the View menu.
2. Select the view you want: Large Icons, Small Icons, List, or Details.

Sorting the Contents

1. In the window you want to sort, open the View menu and select the Arrange Icons command.
2. From the submenu, choose the sort order you want.

Using Windows Explorer to View Files and Folders

1. Click the Start button.
2. Select Programs and then Windows Explorer.
3. To expand a folder (see the subfolders within), click the plus sign (+) next to the folder. To collapse the folder and hide these subfolders, click the minus sign (–).
4. To view the contents of a drive or folder, click the item on the left side.

Working in Web View

1. Click the Start button.
2. Select Settings and then Folder Options.
3. Select Web style and click the OK button.

25

Displaying Files and Folders

The most common analogy used to describe files, folders, and hard disks is that of a filing cabinet. You can think of your hard disk as one big filing cabinet. If all your files were lumped together on the hard disk, finding the file you needed would be difficult, if not impossible. Instead, much like a filing cabinet has file folders, a hard disk can be divided into folders. You can then store like files together in a folder. A folder can contain files or other folders.

The folders you have on your system will vary. Usually programs are installed in their own folder, so you probably have a folder for each program on your system. That folder might contain subfolders for different parts of the program. Windows 98, for instance, has its own folder with many subfolders for different items. In addition to the folders already set up on your system, you can create your own folders, as covered later in this part.

When you want to view the folders and files on your system, you can use My Computer. You can then work with the displayed items, as covered in later chapters in this part. If you prefer, you can also use Windows Explorer, also covered here.

Basic Survival

Using My Computer to Display Files

You can use My Computer to browse through the drives and folders on your system. The contents of each drive or folder are displayed in a separate window. Most novices prefer this method. Follow these steps:

1. Double-click the My Computer icon on your desktop. You see icons for each drive on your system, as well as some system folders.

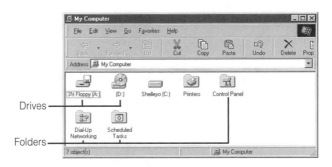

Drives
Folders

You can set
up Windows
so that each
window is
closed when a
new one is
opened. To
make this
change, click
Start,
Settings,
Folder Options.
Make the
change and
then click OK.

2. Double-click the drive you want to open.

3. Double-click the folder you want to open.

4. Continue double-clicking folders until you find the folder or file you want to work with. Notice that the taskbar displays a button for each open window.

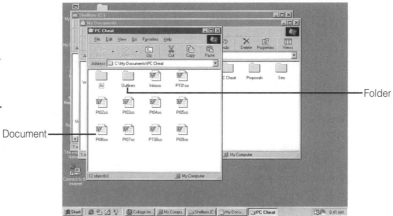

Document
Folder

5. To close a window, click its Close button.

Changing the View

Most of the time, the contents of a file window are displayed as large icons. You can also select to view them as small icons, as a list, or as a detailed list with file dates and sizes. Follow these steps to try another view:

1. In the window, open the View menu. You see a list of different view options.

2. Select the view you want: Large Icons, Small Icons, List, or Details. The contents are displayed in that view. The following figure shows a Details view of a file window.

Shortcut: Use the Views button in the toolbar to change views.

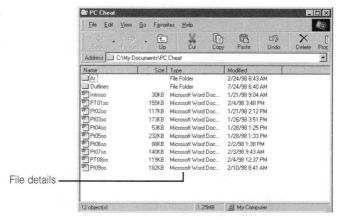

File details —————

Keep in mind that this change affects only the current window.

Beyond Survival

Sorting the Contents

You can sort the contents of a window so that you can more easily find the files you want. Windows enables you to arrange the files in a folder by name, type, date, and size. Sorting the files is even easier if you choose to view them by the file details first. In this view, you can simply click the column heading to sort the files by that heading (for example, click Size to sort by size).

Follow these steps:

1. Open the window you want to sort, and change to the view you want.

2. Open the View menu and select the Arrange Icons command.

3. From the submenu, choose the sort order you want. Windows sorts the files in the selected order. The following figure shows a detailed view of a file window sorted by modified date.

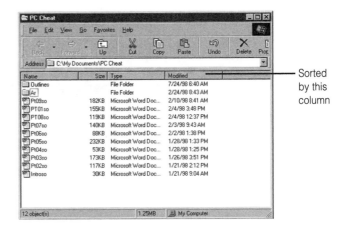

Sorted by this column

Using Windows Explorer

You can also use Windows Explorer; this program presents your system contents in a hierarchical structure in a two-column window. The left pane displays all the drives and folders on your system. The right pane displays the contents of the selected drive or folder from the left. Because you can see the entire system in one window, some users prefer this method. You can try both and see which you prefer. Follow these steps to start Windows Explorer:

1. Click the Start button.

2. Select Programs and then Windows Explorer. The program is started, and you see the contents of your system in a hierarchical view.

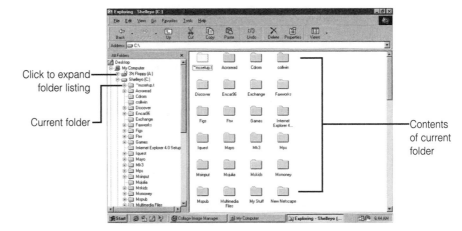

Click to expand folder listing

Current folder

Contents of current folder

3. To expand a folder (see the subfolders within), click the plus sign (+) next to the folder. To collapse the folder and hide these subfolders, click the minus sign ([ms]).

4. To view the contents of a drive or folder, click the item on the left side. The right side shows the contents of that selected item.

Working in Web View

New with Windows 98 is the capability to browse the contents of your system, much like browsing a Web page. Instead of double-clicking to open an icon, you can simply click once. Follow these steps to use this view:

1. Click the Start button.

2. Select Settings and then Folder Options. You see the General tab of the Folder Options dialog box.

Use this tab to set folder options

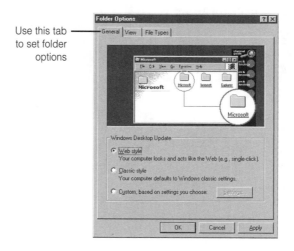

3. Select Web style and click the OK button. The contents of your system are displayed as links. You can click the icon to open it.

Single-click
to open an
icon

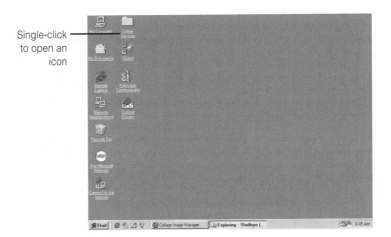

You can also use Active Desktop to view Web content on your desktop. For information on this topic as well as on using the Channel bar, see Part VII, "Getting Connected to the Internet."

Cheat Sheet

Creating a New Folder

1. Open the drive or folder where you want to place the new folder.

2. Open the File menu and select the New command.

3. In the submenu that appears, select Folder.

4. Type a name for the new folder and press Enter.

Deleting a Folder

1. Right-click the folder and select the Delete command.

2. Click the Yes button to confirm the deletion.

Renaming a Folder

1. Right-click the folder you want to rename.

2. Select the Rename command.

3. Type the new name and press Enter.

Moving Folders

1. Start Windows Explorer.

2. In the right pane, display the folder you want to move.

3. In the left pane, display the folder or drive where you want to move the folder.

4. Drag the folder to the new location.

Copying Folders

1. Start Windows Explorer.

2. In the right pane, display the folder you want to copy.

3. In the left pane, display the folder or drive where you want to place the copy.

4. Hold down the Ctrl key and then drag the folder you want to copy to the location where you want to place the copy.

26

Creating New Folders

To keep your files organized, you should create folders for them. The organization and names for your folders are up to you. You might want to use the My Documents folder and set up subfolders for different program types (Word documents, Excel worksheets, and so on). Or you might set up folders for each project or each person who uses your PC. You can select whatever method you prefer.

Basic Survival

Creating a New Folder

To create a new folder, follow these steps:

1. Open the drive or folder where you want to place the new folder. You can open the folder via My Computer or by selecting the folder in the Windows Explorer window.

2. Open the File menu and select the New command. In the submenu that appears, select Folder. Windows adds a new folder (named New Folder) to the window. The name is highlighted so that you can type a more descriptive name.

Type a folder name ——

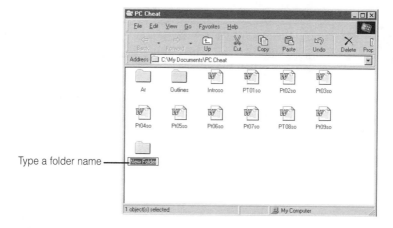

3. Type a name for the new folder and press Enter. The folder is added.

Renaming a Folder

If you don't like the name you used when you first created a folder, you can change it. You can type up to 255 characters, including spaces. To rename a folder, follow these steps:

Use a descriptive name.

1. Right-click the folder you want to rename. (You can display the folder by using either My Computer or Windows Explorer.)

2. Select the Rename command. The name is highlighted so that you can type a new name or edit the existing name.

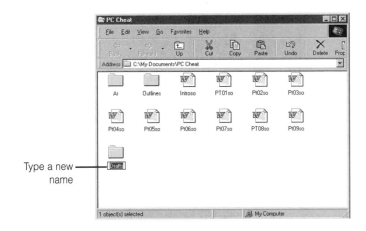

Type a new name

3. Type the new name and press Enter.

Deleting a Folder

If you create a folder you no longer need, you can delete it. Windows deletes the folder and all its contents. Follow these steps:

Check the folder contents before you delete it.

1. Right-click the folder using either My Computer or Windows Explorer.

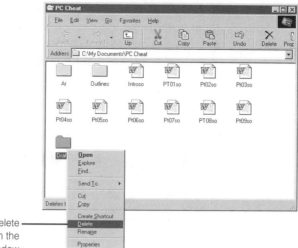

2. Select the Delete command.

3. Click the Yes button to confirm the deletion. The folder
and all of its contents are deleted.

If you make a mistake, you can undo the deletion using the
Edit, Undo command. Alternatively, you can retrieve the item
from the trash as covered in Chapter 27, "Selecting Files."

Beyond Survival

**Moving
Folders**

As you work with your computer more and more, you might
need to do some reorganizing. For instance, you might set up
new folders and want to move existing folders (and their contents) around. You can move a folder using My Computer or
Windows Explorer, but Windows Explorer is the best tool
because you can simply drag the folder from its current location to the new one. Follow these steps:

1. Display the folder you want to move. Remember that
you click a folder on the left to display its contents in the
pane on the right. Also, you can expand the folder listing
by clicking the plus sign (+) next to any of the listed
folders.

If the folders are close to each other, you can display them both in the left pane. If they are far apart in the overall list, you can display the folder to move on the right side and then drag to the left.

2. In the left pane, display the folder or drive where you want to move the folder. You can simply expand or scroll the list to display the folder or drive you want.

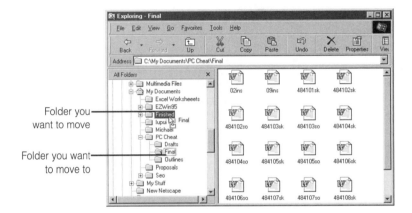

Folder you
want to move

Folder you want
to move to

3. Drag the folder to the new location. The folder and its contents are moved.

**Copying
Folders**

You can make a copy of a folder and all its contents. For instance, you might want to copy an important folder so that you have a backup copy. (For more information on backing up, see Part VI, "Maintaining Your System.") It's easier to copy a folder using Windows Explorer, so start Windows Explorer and then follow these steps:

1. In the right pane, display the folder you want to copy.

2. In the left pane, display the folder or drive where you want to place the copy. You can simply expand or scroll the list to display the folder or drive you want.

3. Hold down the Ctrl key and then drag the folder you want to copy to the location where you want to place the copy. The folder and its contents are copied.

Cheat Sheet

Selecting a File

1. Click the file.

Selecting Several Files in a Row

1. Click the first file.
2. Hold down the Shift key and click the last file.

Selecting Several Files Not in a Row

1. Click the first file.
2. Hold down the Ctrl key and then click each other file yo want to select.

Selecting All Files

1. Open the Edit menu.
2. Select the Select All command.

Deselecting a File

1. Click outside the file.

27

Selecting Files

The preceding chapter covered how to work with folders, but you also will want to work with individual files or groups of files. For instance, you might want to delete a group of files or copy a file from a folder to a floppy disk. The first step when working with files is to select the files you want, as covered in this chapter. You can select a single file or a group of files.

Basic Survival

Selecting and Deselecting a File

To select a single file, click it. The file is selected. To deselect a file, click outside it.

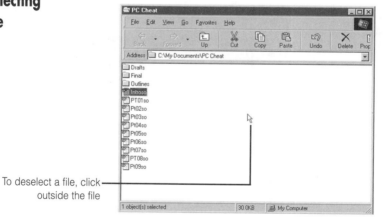

To deselect a file, click outside the file

Selecting Several Files

For other tasks, you might want to work with several files. For instance, you might want to print several files or copy several files to a floppy disk. You can select files that are next to each other, files that are not next to each other, or all files.

To select several files in a row, follow these steps:

1. Click the first file.

2. Hold down the Shift key and click the last file.

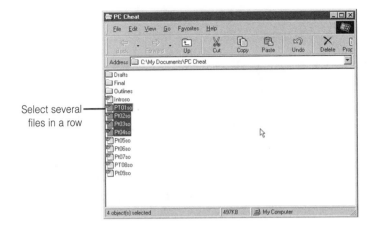

Select several
files in a row

If the files aren't next to each other, use another method for selecting multiple files. Follow these steps:

1. Click the first file.

2. Hold down the Ctrl key and then click each other file you want to select.

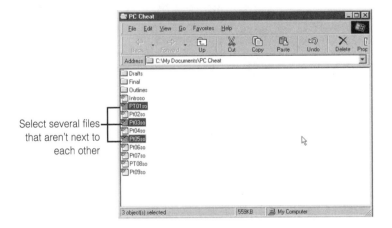

Select several files
that aren't next to
each other

In some cases, you might want to select all files in a particular window. You can do so by following these steps:

1. Open the Edit menu.

2. Click the Select All command.

146

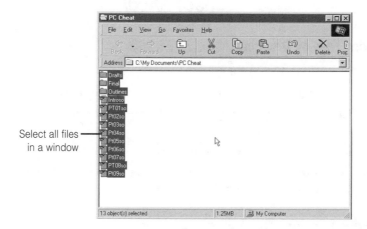

Select all files
in a window

**Inverting a
Selection**

Beyond Survival

You can invert a selection (select all files that are unselected and deselect all selected files). To do this, open the Edit menu and select the Invert Selection command.

Cheat Sheet

Moving Files by Dragging

1. Start Windows Explorer.
2. In the right pane, display the files you want to move.
3. Scroll the left pane until you see the folder to which you want to move the files.
4. Select the files you want to move.
5. Hold down the mouse button and drag the files to the new folder in the left pane of the window.

Copying Files from One Folder to Another

1. Start Windows Explorer.
2. Display the files you want to copy on the right side of the window.
3. Select the files you want to copy.
4. On the left side, scroll through the window until you can see the drive or folder in which you want to place the copies.
5. Hold down the Ctrl key and drag the selected files to the drive or folder where you want to place the copies.

Copying Files from Your Hard Disk to a Floppy Disk

1. Insert the floppy disk into the drive.
2. Display the files you want to copy using either My Computer or Windows Explorer.
3. Select the files you want to copy.
4. Right-click the files.
5. From the shortcut menu, select Send To and then select your floppy drive (usually drive A).

28

Moving and Copying Files

When keeping your files organized, you might need to move a file or files from one location to another. For example, you might decide to use a different organization, or maybe you inadvertently saved a document in the wrong folder, or perhaps your projects have grown so much you need to reorganize your files and put them in different folders.

Copying is similar to moving, but instead of one version of the selected file, you end up with two. For instance, you might need to copy all the files in a folder so that you have extra copies in case something happens to the originals. You might want to copy a file to a floppy disk so that you can take the file with you.

The easiest way to move and copy files is to use Windows Explorer. This program works better than My Computer because you can drag and drop the file all in one window. You can also use a command method, covered later in this chapter.

Basic Survival

**Moving
Files**

To move a file or group of files from one folder to another, follow these steps:

1. Start Windows Explorer.

2. In the right pane, display the files you want to move.

3. Scroll the left pane until you see the folder to which you want to move the files.

4. Select the files you want to move.

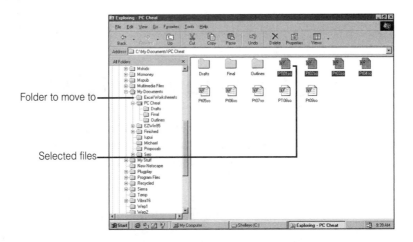

Folder to move to

Selected files

5. Hold down the mouse button and drag the files to the new folder in the left pane of the window. The files are moved.

If you make a mistake, you can undo the move by choosing the Undo command from the Edit menu.

Copying Files from One Folder to Another

Moving files deletes the selected files from one folder or drive and then copies them to another folder or drive. In some cases, you might want to have two copies of the files—that is, leave the files in the original location and copy them to another drive or folder.

To copy from one folder to another using Windows Explorer, follow these steps:

1. Start Windows Explorer.

2. Display the files you want to copy on the right side of the window. Select these files.

3. On the left side, scroll through the window until you can see the drive or folder in which you want to place the copies.

4. Hold down the Ctrl key and drag the selected files to the drive or folder where you want to place the copy. You can tell that you are copying because the mouse pointer displays a little plus sign.

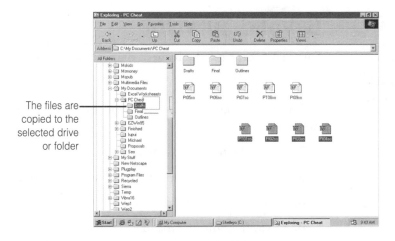

The files are
copied to the
selected drive
or folder

Copying Files from Your Hard Disk to a Floppy Disk

The easiest way to copy from your hard disk to a floppy disk is to use the Send To command. Follow these steps:

1. Insert the floppy disk into the drive.

2. Display the files you want to copy using either My Computer or Windows Explorer.

3. Select the files you want to copy.

4. Right-click the files.

5. From the shortcut menu, select Send To and then select your floppy drive (usually drive A).

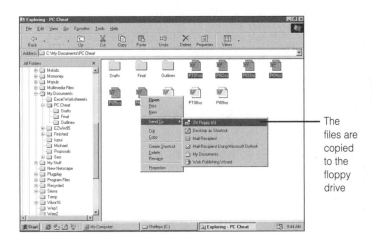

The files are copied to the floppy drive

Beyond Survival

Moving Files with a Command

Some users can't get the hang of dragging and dropping to copy or move a folder. Others might not like working in Windows Explorer. If this is the case for you, you can use a menu command to move files from one folder to another. Follow these steps:

1. Select the files you want to move.

Shortcut: Use the Cut and Paste buttons in the toolbar.

2. Open the Edit menu and select the Cut command.

3. Open the folder where you want to place the files.

4. Open the Edit menu and select the Paste command. The selected files are moved to the new folder.

Copying Files with a Command

Just as you can move files with a command, you can also copy them. Again, you might prefer this method to the drag-and-drop method used with Windows Explorer. Follow these steps:

1. Select the files you want to copy.

2. Open the Edit menu and select the Copy command.

Shortcut: Use the Copy and Paste buttons in the toolbar.

3. Open the folder where you want to place the copied files.

4. Open the Edit menu and select the Paste command. The selected files are copied to the new folder.

Cheat Sheet

Deleting a File

1. Using either My Computer or Windows Explorer, select the files you want to delete.
2. Right-click the selected items and then select the Delete command.
3. When prompted to confirm the deletion, click the Yes button.

Retrieving a Deleted Item from the Recycle Bin

1. On the desktop, double-click the Recycle Bin.
2. Select the items you want to undelete.
3. Right-click the selected items and then select the Restore command.

Emptying the Recycle Bin

1. Double-click the Recycle Bin icon.
2. Check out the contents and be sure that the Recycle Bin does not contain any files or folders you want to keep.
3. Open the File menu and select the Empty Recycle Bin command.
4. Confirm the deletion by clicking the Yes button.

29

Deleting and Undeleting Files

As you use your computer more and more, the files you have will multiply, and eventually you will have to weed out the old, unneeded stuff. Deleting files you don't need frees up the disk space for new files.

When you delete a file or folder, keep in mind that Windows does not really delete the file but simply moves it to the Recycle Bin. You can undo the deletion and recover the item from the Recycle Bin if you make a mistake and delete a file you need. If you want to permanently get rid of the file, empty the Recycle Bin. This chapter covers all these tasks.

You can also clean up unnecessary files using the Disk Cleanup feature, as covered in Chapter 43, "Cleaning Up Files."

Basic Survival

Deleting a File

Follow these steps to delete a file or group of files:

1. Using either My Computer or Windows Explorer, select the files you want to delete.

2. Right-click the selected items and then select the Delete command.

Shortcuts: You can use the Delete button in the toolbar or the Delete key on the keyboard to delete a file or group of files.

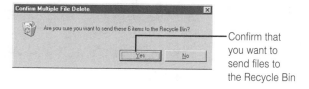

Confirm that you want to send files to the Recycle Bin

3. When prompted to confirm the deletion, click the Yes button.

The file is deleted. If you make a mistake, you can undo the deletion using Edit, Undo. Alternatively, you can retrieve the item from the Recycle Bin, covered next.

Undeleting a File

To retrieve a file from the Recycle Bin and put it back in its original location, follow these steps:

1. On the desktop, double-click the Recycle Bin. You see the contents of this system folder.

2. Select the items you want to undelete.

3. Right-click the selected items and then select the Restore command.

You can also delete items on the desktop by dragging them to the Recycle Bin.

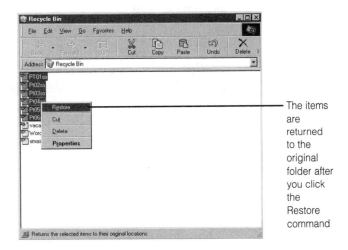

The items are returned to the original folder after you click the Restore command

Beyond Survival

Emptying the Recycle Bin

As mentioned previously, files and folders aren't really deleted with the Delete command, but simply moved to the Recycle Bin, a temporary holding spot. To free up the disk space and really get rid of the files, you must empty the Recycle Bin. Follow these steps:

1. Double-click the Recycle Bin icon.

2. Check out the contents and be sure that the Recycle Bin does not contain any files or folders you want to keep. After you empty the Recycle Bin, you can't get the contents back.

3. When you are sure that you don't need any of the contents, open the File menu and select the Empty Recycle Bin command.

156

Confirm that you
want to remove
the contents of the
Recycle Bin

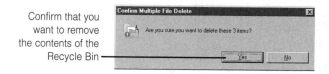

4. Confirm the deletion by clicking the Yes button.

All the files and folders in the Recycle Bin are permanently deleted.

Cheat Sheet

Renaming a File

1. In Windows Explorer or My Computer, display the file you want to rename.
2. Right-click the file and select Rename.
3. Type the new name and press Enter.

30

Renaming Files or Folders

When you save a file, you assign a name. If this name doesn't work—if, for instance, it isn't easy to remember—you can make a change. You can use up to 255 characters, including spaces. You cannot use any of the following characters:

\ ? : * " < > |

In some DOS and Windows applications, the filename or folder name is truncated to the old eight-character limitation. When a program truncates a folder name or filename, it adds a tilde (~) and a number to indicate that the name has been shortened.

Basic Survival

Renaming a File

Follow these steps to rename a file:

1. In Windows Explorer or My Computer, display the file you want to rename.

2. Right-click the file and select Rename from the shortcut menu that appears. Windows highlights the current name and displays a box around it.

Renaming files is easy

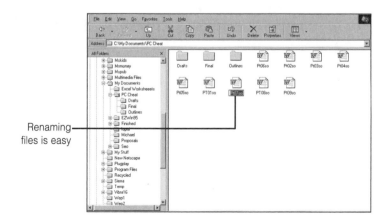

3. Type the new name and press Enter.

Beyond Survival

You can tell a little bit about a file by its name—especially the file extension. This part of the filename can indicate the file type. The following list gives some common file extensions as well as the associated file types:

EXE	Program file (executable)
BAT	Batch file
BMP	Bitmap (image) file
INI	Windows configuration
CPL	Control Panel file
DOC	Word document
XLS	Excel document
TXT	Text file

When you double-click a document file, Windows runs the program associated with that type of file. To view a list of files and associations, follow these steps:

1. Click Start, Settings, Folder Options. You see the Folder Options dialog box.

2. Click the File Types tab.

3. Click any of the file types to see the associated program.

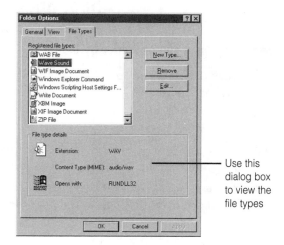

Use this
dialog box
to view the
file types

1. Click Cancel to close the dialog box.

Cheat Sheet

Searching for a File or Folder by Name

1. Click the Start button, choose the Find command, and then choose Files or Folders.
2. Type the name of the file or folder you want to search for in the Named text box.
3. To look on a drive other than the one listed, display the Look In list box and select the drive you want to search.
4. Windows looks in the selected drive and all subfolders on that drive. If you don't want to look in the subfolders, uncheck the Include sub-folders check box.
5. Click the Find Now button.

Searching for a File or Folder by Content

1. Click the Start button, choose the Find command, and then choose Files or Folders.
2. In the Containing text text box, type the text you want to find.
3. To change the drive on which Windows will conduct the search, display the Look In list box and choose the drive you want to search.
4. Click the Find Now button.

Finding Files and Folders by Date

1. Click the Start button, choose the Find command, and then choose Files or Folders.
2. Click the Date tab.
3. Click the Find all files option button.
4. Display the drop-down list next to Find all files and select to find all files modified, created, or accessed within the date range.
5. Select the date range. You can select between and then enter two dates. Alternatively, you can select during a set number of months or days.
6. Click the Find Now button.

31

Searching for Files

After you've worked for months with your applications, your computer will become filled with various folders and files, which can make it nearly impossible for you to know where everything is. Luckily, Windows includes a command that helps you locate specific files or folders. If you know the name, you can search by name. You can also search for a file by its contents or date.

Basic Survival

Searching for a File or Folder by Name

If you know the name of the file or folder but just can't remember where you placed it, you can search for the file by name (or partial name). Follow these steps:

1. Click the Start button, choose the Find command, and then choose Files or Folders.

2. Type the name of the file or folder you want to search for in the Named text box. You can use the characters * and ? (known as *wildcards*) in the search. For example, to find all files ending with the extension .doc, type *.doc. Similarly, you could type chap??.* to find all files beginning with *chap*, followed by any two characters, and ending in any extension.

Enter filename —

Select which —
drive to search

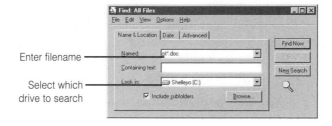

3. To look on a drive different from the one listed, display the Look In list box and select the drive you want to search.

4. Windows looks in the selected drive and all subfolders on that drive. If you don't want to look in the subfolders, uncheck the Include subfolders check box.

5. Click the Find Now button. Windows displays a list of found files and folders at the bottom of the dialog box. You can double-click any of the listed files or folders to go to that file or folder.

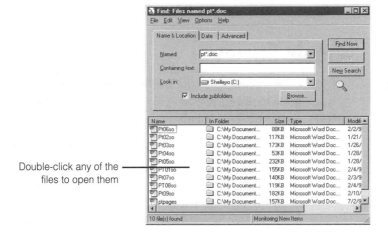

Double-click any of the files to open them

If you want to try a new search, you can clear the existing search entries by clicking the New Search button. Confirm that you want to clear the current search by clicking the OK button in the dialog box that appears.

Searching for a File or Folder by Contents

If you don't know the name of the file or folder you want but you have some idea of what it contains, you can search for it by contents. Pick a unique word or phrase so that you don't end up with too many matches. Follow these steps:

1. Click the Start button, choose the Find command, and then choose Files or Folders.

2. If you want, enter the name of the file you want to search for. You can search on more than one criterion—a file-name and contents, for instance. If you don't want to limit the search, leave the Named text box blank.

3. In the Containing text text box, type the text you want to find.

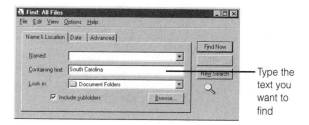

Type the text you want to find

4. To change the drive on which Windows will conduct the search, display the Look In list box and choose the drive you want to search.

5. Click the Find Now button. Windows searches the selected drive and displays a list of found files at the bottom of the dialog box. You can double-click any of the listed files or folders to go to that file or folder.

Double-click any of the listed files

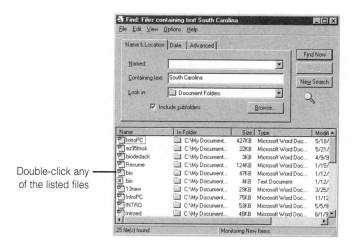

165

Finding Files and Folders by Date

As another search possibility, you can search for files within a particular date range. For instance, suppose that you know you worked on a file this past week, but you can't remember the name. You can display a list of all files worked on within a certain date range. Follow these steps:

1. Click the Start button, choose the Find command, and then choose Files or Folders.

2. If you want to search for both a name and date range, enter the name of the file you want to search for in the Named text box. Leave this blank if you don't want to limit the search.

3. Click the Date tab.

4. Click the Find all files option button. Notice that these options then become available.

5. Display the drop-down list next to Find all files and select to find all files modified, created, or accessed within the date range.

6. Select the date range. You can select between and then enter two dates. Or you can select during a set number of months or days. The settings shown in the following figure will search for all files modified during the previous one day.

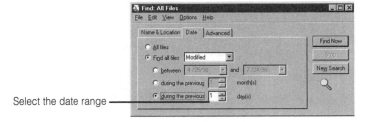

Select the date range

7. Click the Find Now button. Windows searches the selected drive and displays all matching files and folders.

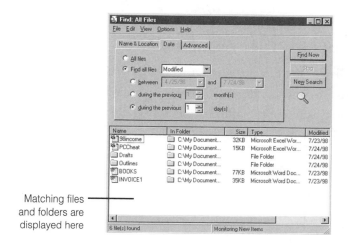

Matching files
and folders are
displayed here

Cheat Sheet

Displaying File or Folder Properties

1. Display the file or folder for which you want information.
2. Right-click the file and choose Properties from the shortcut menu.
3. Review any of the information.
4. Click the OK button.

Displaying Disk Properties

1. Open My Computer to display the drives on your system.
2. Right-click the drive and choose Properties from the shortcut menu.
3. Review the information.
4. Click the OK button.

Viewing System Properties

1. Right-click the My Computer icon.
2. Select Properties from the shortcut menu.
3. Review any of the information.
4. Click the OK button.

32

Displaying Disk Properties

Shortcut:
Select the
file or folder
and then click
the
Properties
button in the
toolbar.

Sometimes you might see a file or folder on your system and not know how it got there. What does the file contain? When was it added? You can get information about the file or folder by viewing its properties. You can also view properties about your hard disk, such as how much space is left. And for really detailed information, you can view the properties of your system.

Basic Survival

**Displaying
File
Properties**

When you want detailed information about a particular file—including the type of file; where it is stored; its size; and creation, modification, and access dates—view the file properties. Follow these steps:

1. Display the file for which you want information.

2. Right-click the file and choose Properties from the shortcut menu.

3. Review any of the information. Depending on the file type, you might see different tabs. You can click any of the tabs to view that information.

This tab provides general information about the selected file

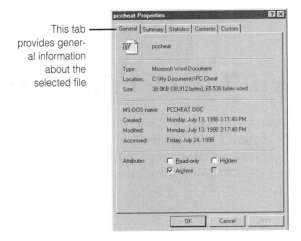

4. Click the OK button.

Displaying Folder Properties

A folder properties dialog box is similar to a file one, but you see the number of files and folders that the folder contains. You also see only the creation date. Follow these steps to view a folder's properties:

1. Display the folder for which you want information.

2. Right-click the folder and choose Properties from the shortcut menu.

3. Review the information.

This window provides general information about the selected folder

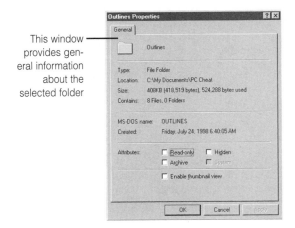

4. Click the OK button.

Displaying Disk Properties

You can display a disk's properties when you want to see the size of the disk and how much free space you have. Use this command also to access disk tools (covered in Part VI, "Maintaining Your System"). Follow these steps:

1. Open My Computer to display the drives on your system. (If you want to view the properties of a floppy disk, insert that disk.)

2. Right-click the drive and choose Properties from the shortcut menu.

3. Review the information.

This tab provides general information about the selected disk ——

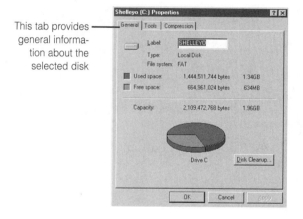

4. Click the OK button.

Beyond Survival

Viewing System Properties

System properties display some high-tech information about your system such as devices that are set up and hardware profiles. You might need to review this information if you are troubleshooting a problem such as a device that is not working properly. Another reason to view this information is to see

171

which version of Windows you are running; that information is displayed on the General tab. To view system properties, follow these steps:

1. Right-click the My Computer icon.

2. Select Properties from the shortcut menu.

3. Review the information.

This window
provides
general
information
about the
system

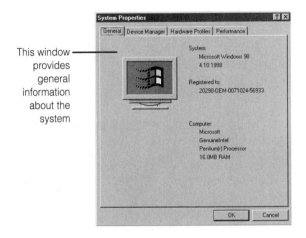

4. Click the OK button.

PART
5

Customizing Windows

After you become more comfortable with Windows, you may want to make some changes to how it works. Some changes are purely personal; you might add a wallpaper image, for instance, because you like it. Other changes may help speed your work. For instance, if you are left-handed, you can change the primary mouse button. The following topics are covered:

- Customizing Windows
- Changing How the Desktop Looks
- Using a Screen Saver
- Viewing Web Content on Your Desktop
- Changing the Taskbar
- Changing the System Date and Time
- Changing How the Mouse and Keyboard Work
- Playing Sounds for Key Windows Actions
- Configuring Windows for Special Needs

Cheat Sheet

Wallpapering Your Desktop

1. Right-click the desktop and select Properties.
2. In the Wallpaper list, select the wallpaper you want to use.
3. Click the OK button.

Using a Pattern for the Desktop

1. Right-click the desktop and select Properties.
2. Click the Pattern button.
3. Click the pattern you want to use.
4. Click the OK button.
5. Click the OK button.

Using a Different Color Scheme

1. Right-click the desktop and select Properties.
2. Click the Appearance tab.
3. Display the Scheme drop-down list box and select the color scheme you want to use.
4. Click the OK button.

Changing How the Icons Are Displayed

1. Right-click the desktop and select Properties.
2. Click the Effects tab.
3. Check any of the visual effects you want to turn on. Uncheck any effects you want to turn off.
4. To change the icon used for a desktop icon, select the icon and then click the Change Icon button. In the Change Icon dialog box, select the icon you want to use and click OK.
5. Click the OK button.

33

Changing How the Desktop Looks

The desktop is the background of the Windows screen. If you don't like the plain background, you can make some changes. You can use wallpaper, use a pattern, change the color scheme, and change how the icons are displayed, as covered in this section. You can also select a different resolution (or screen area).

Basic Survival

Wall-papering Your Desktop

Windows comes with several wallpaper designs that it installs in the \WINDOWS folder. You can select from several different wallpaper styles including bubbles, circles, houndstooth, and more. Follow these steps to select a wallpaper for the desktop:

1. Right-click the desktop and select Properties from the shortcut menu that appears. The Display Properties dialog box appears, with the Background tab selected.

2. In the Wallpaper list, select the wallpaper you want to use. You see a preview of how the wallpaper will look on the sample monitor.

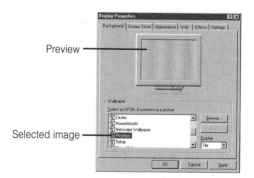

Preview

Selected image

3. If you see only a small image in the center, the image is centered. Open the Display drop-down list and select Tile.

4. When you find the wallpaper you want to use, click OK. The wallpaper is added to the desktop.

If you change your mind and want to turn off the wallpaper, follow the same steps, but select (None) from the Wallpaper list.

Using a Pattern

If you can't find a wallpaper you like, you can try the patterns. You can use any of several predesigned patterns including bricks, buttons, cargo net, daisies, and others.

Note that you can select a pattern or wallpaper, but not both. To select a pattern, you must have wallpaper set to None.

Follow these steps to add a pattern to the desktop:

1. Right-click the desktop and select Properties from the shortcut menu that appears. The Display Properties dialog box appears, with the Background tab selected.

2. Click the Pattern button. You see the Pattern dialog box.

3. Click the pattern you want to use. You see a preview of the selected pattern.

4. When you find the pattern you want, click OK.

In the Display Properties dialog box, you see a preview of the selected pattern.

Selected pattern ——— Preview

5. Click the OK button to use this pattern.

If you change your mind and want to turn off the pattern, follow the same steps, but select (None) from the Pattern list.

Using a Different Color Scheme

You can also customize the colors used for onscreen elements, including the active title bar, desktop, application background, or menus. The easiest way is to use one of the predefined color schemes. To do so, follow these steps:

1. Right-click the desktop and select Properties from the shortcut menu. The Display Properties dialog box appears.

2. Click the Appearance tab. You see the current scheme as well as how each element appears in this selected scheme.

Select a new scheme from this list

3. Display the Scheme drop-down list box and select the color scheme you want to use. You see a preview of how the desktop will look using this new scheme.

4. Click OK. Windows uses the selected scheme for all onscreen elements.

If you change your mind and want to go back to the original colors, follow the same steps; select Windows Standard from the Scheme drop-down list.

Changing How the Icons Are Displayed

Another change you can make to how your desktop appears is to change the look of the icons. You can select visual effects such as large icons, animated windows, and other changes. Follow these steps:

1. Right-click the desktop and select Properties from the shortcut menu. The Display Properties dialog box appears.

2. Click the Effects tab.

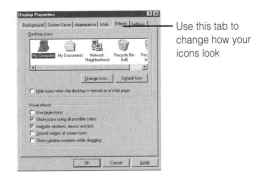

Use this tab to change how your icons look

3. Check any of the visual effects you want to turn on. Uncheck any effects you want to turn off.

4. To change the icon used for a desktop icon, select the icon and then click the Change Icon button. In the Change Icon dialog box, select the icon you want to use and click OK.

5. Click the OK button. Windows makes the changes to the desktop icons.

If you change your mind and want to go back to the original icon, follow the same steps. Select the icon you want to change and then click the Default Icon button.

Changing the Screen Area

If you want to change the number of colors used in your display or the size of the screen area, follow these steps:

1. Right-click the desktop and select Properties from the shortcut menu. The Display Properties dialog box appears.

2. Click the Settings tab.

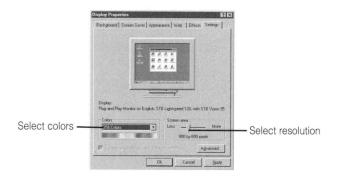

Select colors ————— Select resolution

3. Display the Colors drop-down list and select the number of colors to use for the display.

4. To change the screen area, drag the Screen area slider bar left or right to make the size of the items (resolution) larger or smaller.

5. Click the OK button.

6. When prompted, click OK. You see how the screen looks using the new settings, and Windows prompts you to confirm the change.

7. Click the Yes button. Windows makes the changes.

Beyond Survival

Using Another File for the Wallpaper

You aren't limited to the wallpaper files included with Windows. You can use other graphic file types as the wallpaper image. You can select, for instance, an image from the Web to use as your wallpaper. Follow these steps:

1. Right-click the desktop and select Properties from the shortcut menu that appears. The Display Properties dialog box appears, with the Background tab selected.

2. Click the Browse button. You see the Browse dialog box, which displays all background file types.

179

Open a background file from this dialog

3. Select the file you want to use and click the Open button.

4. If necessary, change how the image is displayed by opening the Display drop-down list and selecting Tile, Center, or Stretch. You see a preview of the image (shown here is my favorite tennis player, Patrick Rafter, at Wimbledon).

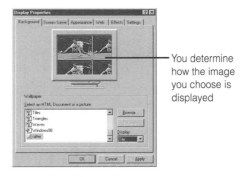

You determine how the image you choose is displayed

5. Click the OK button. The wallpaper is added to the desktop.

Editing the Pattern

If you don't like any of the patterns, create your own. You can edit the repeating pattern that is used by following these steps:

1. Right-click the desktop and select Properties from the shortcut menu that appears. The Display Properties dialog box appears, with the Background tab selected.

2. Click the Pattern button. You see the Pattern dialog box.

3. Click the pattern you want to start with. You start with an existing pattern and then edit it. Select a pattern that is closest to what you want.

4. Click the Edit Pattern button. You see the Pattern Editor.

Type the pattern name here

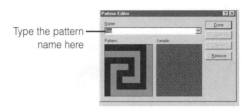

5. Type a name for this new pattern.

6. Edit the pattern. Click a box to change its color from green to black or vice versa. You see the pattern and how the desktop will look with the pattern as you edit.

Your pattern —————— ——— The desktop using this pattern

7. When you are finished making changes, click Done. Click the Yes button to save the pattern. When you return to the Pattern dialog box, your pattern is selected.

8. Click OK to close the Pattern dialog box.

9. Click OK to close the Display Properties dialog box.

Changing Individual Colors

If none of the predefined color schemes suit your fancy, design your own. You can select the color used for each onscreen item. You can also save the set of colors as your own personalized color scheme. Follow these steps:

1. Right-click the desktop and select Properties from the shortcut menu. The Display Properties dialog box appears.

181

2. Click the Appearance tab. You see the current scheme as well as how each element appears in this selected scheme.

3. Click the item you want to modify in the sample area. For instance, to change the color of the Active Window title bar, click it. You see the name of the item and the settings used for size, color, and font.

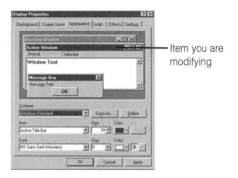

Item you are modifying

4. Make any changes to the color, font, size, and other options. (These will vary depending on what type of item you have selected.)

5. Follow steps 3 and 4 for each item you want to change.

6. To save your selected settings, click the Save As button. Type a name for the scheme and click OK.

7. Click OK to use the new scheme.

Cheat Sheet

Using a Screen Saver

1. Right-click the desktop and select Properties.
2. Click the Screen Saver tab.
3. Display the Screen Saver drop-down list and select the screen saver you want.
4. In the Wait text box, enter the number of minutes you want Windows to wait before displaying the image.
5. Click the OK button.

Stopping a Screen Saver

Move the mouse or press any key on the keyboard.

Using a Password

1. Right-click the desktop and select Properties.
2. Click the Screen Saver tab.
3. Display the Screen Saver drop-down list and select the screen saver you want.
4. In the Wait text box, enter the number of minutes you want Windows to wait before displaying the image.
5. Check the Password Protected check box and then click the Change button.
6. Type the password twice, once in each text box.
7. Click OK.
8. When prompted that the password has been set, click OK.
9. Click OK.

34

Using a Screen Saver

If you left an image onscreen for a long time on older PC monitors, that image could become burned in. (You can sometimes see a burned-in image on ATM machines.) To prevent burn-in, someone came up with the idea of a screen saver. If you didn't use your computer for a certain period of time, the computer would automatically display an animated graphic, which would prevent burn-in.

Today's monitors don't have burn-in problems, but some users still use a screen saver, mostly for show. If you don't use your PC for a certain amount of time, Windows displays a moving graphic image. Windows includes several screen savers you can try.

Basic Survival

Using a Screen Saver

Follow these steps to use a screen saver:

1. Right-click the desktop and select Properties from the shortcut menu. The Display Properties dialog box appears.

2. Click the Screen Saver tab.

To see a preview, click the Preview button.

3. Display the Screen Saver drop-down list and select the screen saver you want.

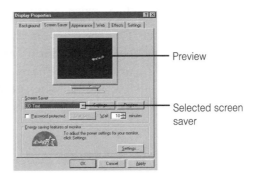

Preview

Selected screen saver

4. In the Wait text box, enter the number of minutes you want Windows to wait before displaying the image.

5. Click OK.

Windows will display the screen saver after the allotted wait time of inactivity has passed. To stop the screen saver and return to your program, press any key or move the mouse.

Press any key to stop the screen saver.

If you want to turn off the screen saver, follow these same steps, but select None from the Screen Saver drop-down list.

Beyond Survival

Using a Password

You can add a tiny bit of system security by assigning a password. Anyone who tries to deactivate the screen saver will have to type the password. Keep in mind that you can always reboot the computer to get past the screen saver, so this security isn't all that secure.

To assign a password, follow these steps:

1. Right-click the desktop and select Properties from the shortcut menu. The Display Properties dialog box appears.

2. Click the Screen Saver tab.

3. Display the Screen Saver drop-down list and select the screen saver you want.

4. In the Wait text box, enter the number of minutes you want Windows to wait before displaying the image.

5. Check the Password Protected check box and then click the Change button.

6. Type the password twice: once to set the password in the New Password text box and once to confirm the password in the Confirm New Password text box. Click the OK button. When prompted that the password has been set, click OK.

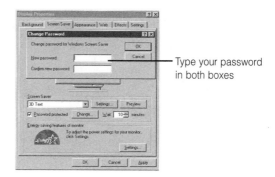

Type your password in both boxes

7. In the Display Properties dialog box, click OK to use the screen saver with the password.

When you set a password and want to deactivate the screen saver, Windows displays the Windows Screen Saver dialog box. Type your password and click OK.

Changing Screen Saver Options

You can modify how the screen saver appears. For instance, you can change the text used for the 3D Text screen saver, or select a speed for some of the patterns. (Depending on the screen saver, the options will vary.) Follow these steps:

1. Right-click the desktop and select Properties from the shortcut menu. The Display Properties dialog box appears.

2. Click the Screen Saver tab.

3. Display the Screen Saver drop-down list and select the screen saver you want.

4. In the Wait text box, enter the number of minutes you want Windows to wait before displaying the image.

5. Click the Settings button. Make any changes to the settings. The following figure shows the options you can select for 3D Text. Click the OK button.

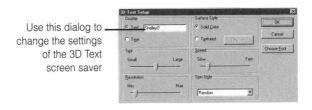

Use this dialog to change the settings of the 3D Text screen saver

6. Click OK to close the Display Properties dialog box.

Cheat Sheet

Viewing Active Desktop

1. Right-click a blank area of the desktop and then select Properties.
2. Click the Web tab.
3. Check the View My Active Desktop as a Web Page check box.
4. To display the Channel bar, check Internet Explorer Channel Bar.
5. Click the OK button.

Viewing Channels

1. In the Channel bar, click the category you want to view.
2. To see a preview, click the channel.
3. Click the Connect button and then follow your logon procedures to get connected to the Internet.
4. From the preview page, click Add Active Channel.
5. In the Modify Channel Usage dialog box, select how to handle the channel subscription.
6. Click the OK button.

35

Viewing Your Desktop as a Web Page

You can also use the Folder Options to set up how folders are displayed. See Part V, "Customizing Windows," for working in Web view for folders.

Viewing Active Desktop

If you have used the Internet, you may be comfortable with that method for viewing content. When you browse content, you can click a link to display the contents. You can set up your desktop to browse its contents just like a Web page. You also can display Web channels, which you can use to browse the Internet. (For more on browsing the Internet, see Part VII, "Getting Connected to the Internet.")

Basic Survival

The name of the feature used to browse Internet content from your desktop is called Active Desktop. You can turn this feature on and then browse several channels. Keep in mind that to access content from the Internet, you must be connected. Alternatively, you can download the content for later viewing.

Follow these steps:

1. Right-click a blank area of the desktop and then select Properties.

2. Click the Web tab.

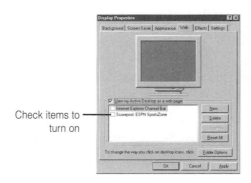

Check items to turn on

3. Check the View my Active Desktop as a Web Page check box.

4. To display the Channel bar, check Internet Explorer Channel Bar.

5. Click the OK button.

The desktop is displayed with the Channel bar.

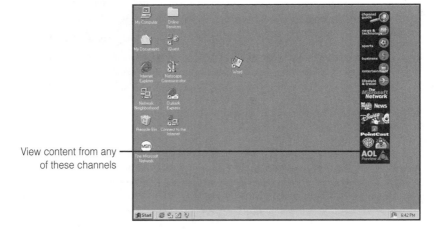

View content from any of these channels

To go back to the regular desktop, right-click a blank area of the desktop, choose Active Desktop, and uncheck View As Web Page by choosing this command.

Beyond Survival

Viewing Channels

Web channels are sites specifically designed for Internet Explorer. You can have content from any of these channels delivered right to your desktop. The Channel bar includes a channel guide, the channels you have set up (and some that are set up for you such as MSNBC News), and several categories, each with different channels. To view the other available channels, follow these steps:

1. Click the category you want to view. Windows displays the available channels in the category (in this example, I chose to view the sports category).

Click any of the listed channels to see a preview of that channel

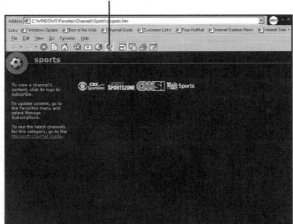

2. To see a preview, click the channel. You are prompted to connect to the Internet.

3. Click Connect and then follow your logon procedures to connect to the Internet. You see the preview page for the selected channel.

4. Click the Add Active Channel button to add the channel to the Channel bar and set up your subscription. You see the Modify Channel Usage dialog box. Here you can select how to handle the channel subscription.

You can also add the channel to the desktop. To do so, click the Add to Active Desktop button and then follow the steps for setting up the channel for the desktop.

Specify your subscription preferences in this dialog box ———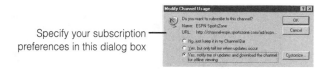

5. Select whether you just want the channel in the Channel bar, whether you want to subscribe and be notified when changes occur, or whether you want to subscribe, be notified, and automatically download content.

6. Click the OK button. The channel is added to your desktop.

To unsubscribe, open the Favorites menu in any Internet Explorer window. Then select Manage Subscriptions. You see the Subscriptions list. Right-click the channel you want to unsubscribe from and select Delete. Confirm the deletion.

Cheat Sheet

Moving the Taskbar

1. Click a blank area of the taskbar and hold down the mouse button.
2. Drag the taskbar to another edge of the screen.

Resizing the Taskbar

1. Position the mouse pointer on the taskbar edge that borders the desktop.
2. Drag the border to the size you want.

Selecting Taskbar Options

1. Open the Start menu, select Settings, and select Taskbar.
2. Make any changes to the options.
3. Click OK.

Changing the Taskbar

The taskbar is within easy reach right at the bottom of your screen. If you don't want it displayed or if you want to move it to a different location, you can do so. You can also change how the taskbar appears.

Basic Survival

Moving the Taskbar

To move the taskbar, follow these steps:

1. Click a blank area of the taskbar and hold down the mouse button.

2. Drag the taskbar to another edge of the screen.

When you release the mouse button, the taskbar appears in the new location.

Drag and drop the taskbar to move it

Resizing the
Taskbar

To resize the taskbar, follow these steps:

1. Position the mouse pointer on the taskbar edge that borders the desktop. The pointer becomes a two-headed
arrow.

2. Drag the border to the size you want.

The taskbar is resized.

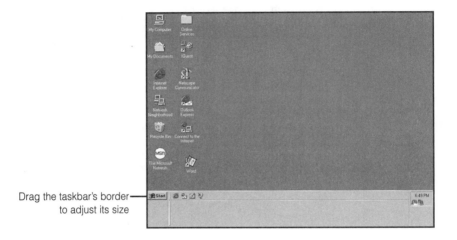

Drag the taskbar's border
to adjust its size

Beyond Survival

Selecting
Taskbar
Options

Follow these steps to set taskbar options:

1. Open the Start menu, select Settings, and select Taskbar.
You see the Taskbar Properties dialog box.

Use this tab to set
taskbar options

2. Make any changes to the following options:

Check the Always On Top option to have the taskbar always appear on top of any other window on the screen.

Check the Auto Hide option to have Windows hide the taskbar from view. You can make the taskbar pop up by moving the mouse pointer to the edge of the screen where the taskbar should appear.

Check Show Small Icons in the Start menu to use smaller icons for items in the Start menu.

Check Show Clock to display the clock; uncheck this option to turn off the clock.

3. Click the OK button.

Cheat Sheet

Changing the Date and Time

1. Right-click the time in the taskbar and select Adjust Date/Time.
2. Make any changes to the date. You can display the Month drop-down list to select a different month and then click the appropriate date on the calendar. Use the Year spin box to increment the year.
3. Make any changes to the time. You can click the time in the clock or use the spin boxes to increment the hour, minutes, or seconds.
4. Click the OK button.

Changing the Time Zone

1. Right-click the time in the taskbar and select Adjust Date/Time.
2. Click the Time Zone tab.
3. Display the drop-down list and select the appropriate time zone.
4. Check whether you want to adjust for daylight savings.
5. Click OK.

Changing Regional Settings

1. Click Start, select Settings, and select Control Panel.
2. Double-click the Regional Settings icon.
3. Display the drop-down list on the Regional Settings tab and select the country.
4. Review (and make changes to, if necessary) each of the other dialog box tabs and their options.
5. Click the OK button.

37

Changing the System Date and Time

Windows uses the system date and time to stamp files. This way you can keep track of when a file was created, modified, accessed, and so on. The current time is also displayed in the taskbar for your convenience. If the date and time are wrong, you can change them.

If you use your computer in another country, you may also want to change the regional settings. These changes affect how dates, times, currency, and numbers are displayed.

Basic Survival

Changing the Date and Time

To change the date and time, follow these steps:

1. Right-click the time in the taskbar and select Adjust Date/Time. You see the Date/Time Properties dialog box.

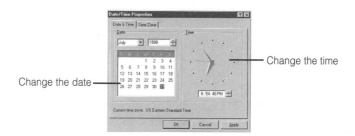

Change the date ———

——— Change the time

2. Make any changes to the date. You can display the Month drop-down list to select a different month and then click the appropriate date on the calendar. Use the Year spin box to increment the year.

3. Make any changes to the time. You can click the time in the clock or use the spin boxes to increment the hour, minutes, or seconds.

4. Click OK.

Beyond Survival

Changing the Date and Time

You can also use the Date/Time Properties dialog box to select a time zone. And you can select whether the clock is automatically adjusted for daylight savings time. Follow these steps:

1. Right-click the time in the taskbar and select Adjust Date/Time. You see the Date/Time Properties dialog box.

2. Click the Time Zone tab.

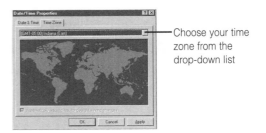

Choose your time zone from the drop-down list

3. Display the drop-down list and select the appropriate time zone.

4. Check whether you want to adjust for daylight savings.

5. Click OK.

Changing Regional Settings

If you are used to a different format for displaying dates, times, or numbers, you may want to select a different regional setting. You can select from several countries and also change each format for individual items (number, currency, date, and time). Follow these steps to make a change:

1. Click Start, select Settings, and select Control Panel. You see the programs in the Control Panel.

2. Double-click the Regional Settings icon. You see the
Regional Settings Properties dialog box.

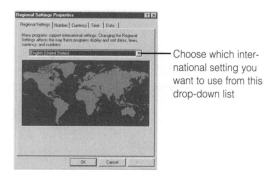

Choose which international setting you want to use from this drop-down list

3. To change to a different country, display the drop-down
list on the Regional Settings tab and select the country.

4. Review (and make changes to, if necessary) each of the
other dialog box tabs and their options.

5. Click OK.

Cheat Sheet

Switching Mouse Buttons

1. Click Start, select Settings, and select Control Panel.
2. Double-click the Mouse icon.
3. In the Button configuration section, select Right-Handed or Left-Handed.
4. If you have trouble double-clicking, adjust the speed by dragging the Double-Click Speed Slider right (slower) or left (faster). You can test the speed by double-clicking the jack-in-the-box.
5. Click OK.

Using Different Pointers

1. Click Start, select Settings, and select Control Panel.
2. Double-click the Mouse icon.
3. Click the Pointers tab.
4. Display the Scheme drop-down list and select the scheme you want to use.
5. Click OK.

Changing the Pointer Speed and Adding a Pointer Trail

1. Click Start, select Settings, and select Control Panel.
2. Double-click the Mouse icon.
3. Click the Motion tab.
4. Make your changes and click OK.

38

Customizing the Mouse

If needed, you can make adjustments to how the mouse works. One change is especially useful if you are left-handed. You can switch the mouse buttons so that you can click the right mouse button for left-clicking and vice versa. You can also adjust the double-click speed, use pointers, and make other changes.

Note that if you have a Microsoft IntelliPoint Mouse, you will see different options. You can select any of the available options for this type of mouse.

You can also make changes to the keyboard settings, including set the repeat rate.

Basic Survival

Switching Mouse Buttons

The most common mouse change is to switch the left and right buttons. Follow these steps to make a change:

1. Click Start, select Settings, and select Control Panel. You see the programs in the Control Panel.

2. Double-click the Mouse icon. You see the Mouse Properties dialog box.

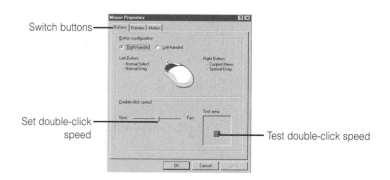

Switch buttons

Set double-click speed

Test double-click speed

3. In the Button configuration section, select Right-Handed or Left-Handed.

4. If you have trouble double-clicking, adjust the speed by dragging the Double-Click Speed Slider right (faster) or left (slower). You can test the speed by double-clicking the jack-in-the-box.

5. Click the OK button.

Customizing the Keyboard

If you have trouble typing on the keyboard, you might want to make a change. You can change the repeat delay (how much time before a key is repeated when you hold it down), the repeat rate (how fast a key is repeated when you hold it down), or the blink rate (how fast the insertion point blinks). Follow these steps to make a change:

1. Click Start, select Settings, and select Control Panel. You see the programs in the Control Panel.

2. Double-click the Keyboard icon. You see the Keyboard Properties dialog box.

Use this dialog to set keyboard properties

3. To change the repeat delay, drag the slider bar to the setting you want.

4. To change the repeat rate, drag the slider bar for Repeat Rate left (Slow) or right (Fast).

Test the repeat rate in the test area.

5. Adjust the cursor blink rate by dragging its slider bar left (slow) or right (fast).

6. Click the OK button.

Beyond Survival

Using Different Mouse Pointers

Another change you can make to the mouse is to select different pointers. For most key actions, the mouse pointer changes its shape to indicate what it is doing. You see one shape, for instance, when the system is busy. You see another shape when you are selecting text. You can select a different set of pointers (called a scheme) by following these steps:

1. Click Start, select Settings, and select Control Panel. You see the programs in the Control Panel.

2. Double-click the Mouse icon. You see the Mouse Properties dialog box.

3. Click the Pointers tab. You see the default set of pointers.

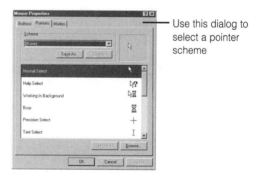

Use this dialog to select a pointer scheme

4. Display the Scheme drop-down list and select the scheme you want to use. You see a preview of each pointer type in the new scheme.

5. Click the OK button.

Changing the Pointer Speed and Adding a Pointer Trail

You can change the pointer speed and add a trail to the pointer. Follow these steps:

1. Click Start, select Settings, and select Control Panel. You see the programs in the Control Panel.

2. Double-click the Mouse icon. You see the Mouse Properties dialog box.

3. Click the Motion tab.

207

Use this dialog to set the pointer speed and the pointer trail

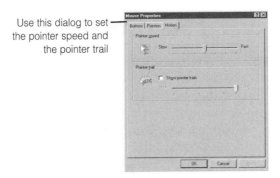

4. Drag the Pointer Speed slider left or right to make it move slower or faster.

5. To show a trail for the pointer, check Show Pointer Trails and then drag the slider bar to select a length.

6. Click OK.

Cheat Sheet

Playing a Sound for a Windows Action

1. Open the Start menu, select Settings, and select Control Panel.
2. Double-click the Sounds icon.
3. To play a sound associated with an event, click the event and then click the Play button.
4. To attach a sound to an event or to change the sound currently attached to an event, click the event in the Events list. Then select a sound file from the Name list.
5. Click OK when you're finished.

Using a Sound Scheme

1. Open the Start menu, select Settings, and select Control Panel.
2. Double-click the Sounds icon. You see the Sounds Properties dialog box.
3. Display the Schemes drop-down list and select the scheme you want to use.
4. To test out the new sounds, click the event you want to try and then click the Play button.
5. Click OK when you're finished.

39

Playing a Sound for Windows Events

You may have noticed that when you make a mistake or click somewhere you shouldn't, you hear a sound. You may also hear sounds for other events. That's because Windows is designed to play a sound when a certain event happens. You can select which events trigger sounds and the sound that is played.

Basic Survival

Assigning a Sound to an Action

You can review the associated sounds Windows plays and make any changes by following these steps:

1. Open the Start menu, select Settings, and select Control Panel.

2. Double-click the Sounds icon. You see the Sounds Properties dialog box. Events that already have sounds attached to them are marked with a speaker icon.

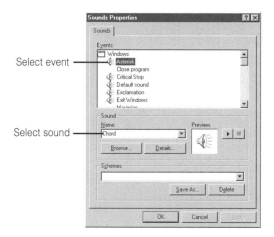

3. To play a sound associated with an event, click the event and then click the Play button.

4. To attach a sound to an event or to change the sound currently attached to an event, click the event in the Events list. Then select a sound file from the Name list.

5. Click OK when you're finished.

Beyond Survival

Using a Sound Scheme

If you want to make several sound changes at once, you can use one of Windows' sound schemes, which are entire sets of sounds for key events. To select a sound scheme, follow these steps:

1. Open the Start menu, select Settings, and select Control Panel.

2. Double-click the Sounds icon. You see the Sounds Properties dialog box.

3. Display the Schemes drop-down list and select the scheme you want to use.

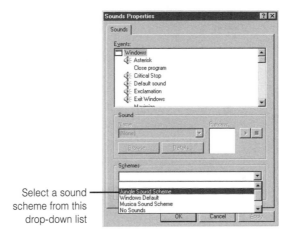

Select a sound scheme from this drop-down list

4. To test out the new sounds, click the event you want to try and then click the Play button.

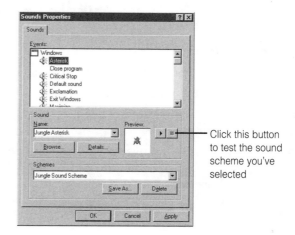

Click this button to test the sound scheme you've selected

If you don't like the sounds, select No Sounds from the Schemes drop-down list.

5. Click OK when you're finished.

To go back to the default scheme, follow the same steps, but select Windows Default from the Schemes drop-down list.

Cheat Sheet

Adding Sounds to Events

1. Open the Start menu, select Settings, and select Control Panel.
2. Double-click the Sounds icon.
3. To play a sound associated with an event, click the event and then click the Play button.
4. To attach a sound to an event or to change the sound currently attached to an event, click the event in the Events list. Then select a sound file from the Name list.
5. Click OK when you're finished.

40

Configuring Windows for Special Needs

If someone who uses your computer has special needs, you can use some of the Windows accessibility options to make Windows easier to use. You can select different options for the keyboard, sound, display, mouse, and general settings.

Basic Survival

Turning On Accessibility Options

The Accessibility dialog box has five tabs, each with settings for certain Windows elements. You can set Keyboard options like StickyKeys, FilterKeys, and ToggleKeys. These are designed to make key combinations easier to press. If you want a visual warning rather than a sound, use the Sound tab. On the Display tab, you can select a high-contrast display for easier reading. If you want to use the keypad instead of the mouse to control the pointer, turn on MouseKeys on the Mouse tab. And finally, the General tab provides options for controlling when the accessibility options are in effect.

To review the available options and if necessary make a change, follow these steps:

1. Open the Start menu, select Settings, and select Control Panel.

2. Double-click the Accessibility Options icon. You see the Accessibility Properties dialog box with the Keyboard tab displayed.

Use this tab to set —— keyboard options

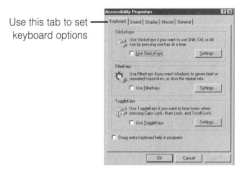

3. Make any changes.

4. To make changes to the sounds, click the Sound tab. Check any of the sound options (SoundSentry or ShowSounds).

Use this tab to set —— sound options

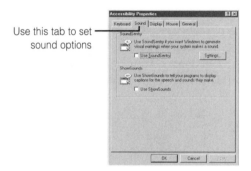

5. To turn on high-contrast display, click the Display tab and check the Use High Contrast check box.

Specify whether you want —— to use the high-contrast option

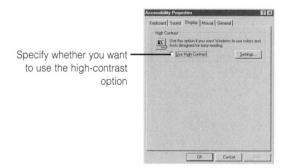

216

6. To use the keypad instead of the mouse, click the Mouse tab and then check Use MouseKeys.

Check this box if you want to control your pointer by using the keypad instead of the mouse

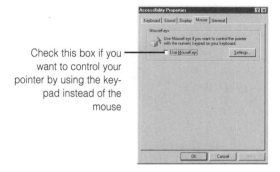

7. To set General options, click the General tab. Make your changes.

Set general accessibility options here

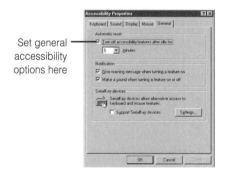

8. Click OK to confirm your changes.

Beyond Survival

Customizing Accessibility Options

You can customize how some of the accessibility options work. If Windows supports customization of an option, you'll see a Settings button next to the option. Follow these steps to make a change:

1. Click the Settings button next to the option you want to customize. You see the available options. The following shows the changes you can make to how StickyKeys works.

This dialog enables you to customize the StickyKeys feature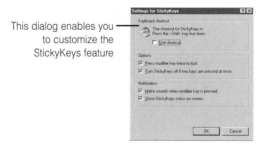

2. Make any changes and click OK.

PART

6

Maintaining Your System

To keep your PC in tip-top shape, you should periodically perform some routine maintenance. Some of these tasks are things you should do every few months. Some are things you need to do if you get new equipment, and finally, some are things you do if you are having problems (or to avoid problems). For all your system maintenance advice, turn to this part, which covers the following topics:

- Maintaining Your System
- Checking for Errors
- Defragmenting Your Disks
- Cleaning up Files
- Creating a Startup Disk
- Backing Up Your System
- Restoring a Backup
- Installing New Hardware
- Setting Up Your Printer
- Scheduling Tasks
- Troubleshooting Problems

Cheat Sheet

Running ScanDisk

1. Double-click the My Computer icon.
2. Right-click the drive you want to check and select the Properties command.
3. Click the Tools tab.
4. Click the Check Now button.
5. Select the type of test. Also, check whether you want to automatically fix errors.
6. Click Start.
7. Click the Close button when the test is complete.

Setting ScanDisk Options

1. In the ScanDisk dialog box, click the Advanced button.
2. For options like Display Summary, Log File, Cross-Linked Files, and Lost File Fragments, select what you want done. You can select one of the options for each set of options.
3. Check or uncheck any of the check box items to turn on (checked) or off (unchecked) that feature.
4. Click OK.
5. Click Start to run the test with the selected options.
6. Click the Close button when the test is complete.

41

Checking for Errors

Maintenance on your hard disk is nothing like maintenance on your car—there is no chassis to lube or oil to change, and there are no spark plugs to replace. In fact, there are no moving parts on your hard disk that you ever need to worry about. But that doesn't mean that you should ignore routine hard disk maintenance.

Hard disk maintenance refers to how your hard disk drive stores files, and steps you need to take to make sure that file storage is done in an efficient manner.

Normally, your hard disk is fairly efficient in the manner in which it stores your files. However, when you delete a file, the file is not actually removed from your hard disk drive. Instead, the file's attributes are changed, indicating that the space used by the file you are deleting is now available (it is now considered "free space") and can be used by other files. Occasionally, though, when a new file is created from this supply of "free space," not all the free space is used by the new file, and the result is a "lost cluster" or "lost chain." A lost cluster (or lost chain) is a portion of a previously deleted file that still appears as if it is being used by that file. It is essentially free space that isn't totally free, and results in a loss of free space on your hard disk drive.

Basic Survival

Running ScanDisk

You can use a utility program called ScanDisk to check you hard disk drive for errors. This program will also automatically fix some types of errors. To run ScanDisk, follow these steps:

1. Double-click the My Computer icon.

2. Right-click the drive you want to check and select the Properties command. You see the Properties dialog box showing the General tab.

3. Click the Tools tab. You see the different tools available for checking your system.

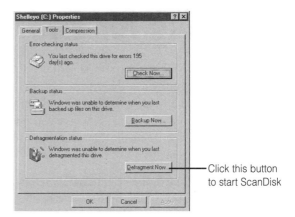

Click this button to start ScanDisk

4. Click the Check Now button. The Windows 98 version of ScanDisk enables you to select the drive you want to check. In addition, you can also choose to perform a Standard check—which checks your files and folders for lost clusters—or a Thorough check, which scans the disk surface for errors.

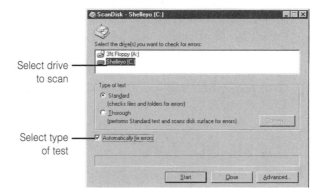

Select drive to scan

Select type of test

5. Select the type of test. Also, check whether you want to automatically fix errors.

6. Click Start. You see the progress of the test. When the test is complete, you see a message box that displays the results of the test.

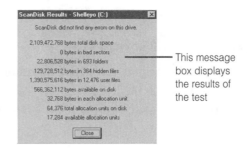

This message box displays the results of the test

7. Click Close.

You can also start ScanDisk from the Start menu. Click Start, Programs, Accessories, System Tools, and then ScanDisk.

Beyond Survival

Setting ScanDisk Options

If you want utmost control over the testing, you can set some advanced options on how the test is run. Follow these steps:

1. In the ScanDisk dialog box, click the Advanced button. You see the ScanDisk Advanced Options dialog box.

This dialog box enables you to set advanced options

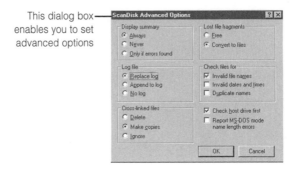

2. For options like Display summary, Log File, Cross-Linked Files, and Lost File Fragments, select what you want done. You can select one of the options for each set of options.

3. Check or uncheck any of the check box items to turn on (checked) or off (unchecked) that feature.

4. Click OK.

5. Click Start to run the test with the selected options.

Cheat Sheet

Defragmenting Your Hard Drive

1. Exit all programs you may have running.
2. Double-click the My Computer icon.
3. Right-click the drive you want to check and select the Properties command.
4. Click the Tools tab.
5. Click the Defragment Now button.
6. When the test is complete, click OK.

Viewing the Defragmenting Progress

If you want to see the results of the defragmenting, you can click the Show Details button. Then click Legend to see what each block represents.

42

Defragmenting Your Disks

Defragmentation is a term most computer users aren't totally familiar with, but it is one you should learn about and decide how it fits into your PC maintenance plans. First, you need to understand how your system stores files.

Your PC's hard disk drives are divided into hundreds of concentric rings; each ring is further divided into storage sections called *clusters*. (Cluster size varies according to which operating system you are running, but the basic idea is the same.) When you store a file on your disk drive, Windows will look for the first empty, or available, cluster it can find to store the file. If the entire file won't fit into one cluster, Windows places the next portion of the file into the next available cluster it finds—even if the clusters aren't adjacent. This process is repeated with as many clusters as are needed to store the file. Windows keeps track of the clusters in which your file is scattered across your disk drive, and can easily re-assemble the file regardless of the number of clusters used to store the file. When you delete files, as you remember from Chapter 29, "Deleting and Undeleting Files," Windows simply makes the clusters that file was stored in available.

After several weeks or months of creating and deleting files and having them scattered all over your hard disk drive, your files become *fragmented*. Windows doesn't have a problem retrieving files, but because the files aren't in adjacent clusters, it does take longer to locate all the parts of file whenever you run a program or open a file to work on.

The good news is that you can rearrange the files on your PC's hard disk so it takes Windows less time to find them. Rearranging your files or their scattered parts is called *defragmentation*.

Defragmenting your files is not essential. You can actually go for years without ever defragmenting your files. But the longer you put it off, the more fragmented your files become and the more time Windows has to spend reassembling your fragmented files. Think of defragmentation as a routine efficiency chore.

Basic Survival

Defrag- menting Your Hard Drive

Windows includes a disk defragmenter that you can use to speed performance of your hard drive. Follow these steps to run this program:

1. Exit all programs you may have running.

2. Double-click the My Computer icon.

3. Right-click the drive you want to check and select the Properties command. You see the Properties dialog box showing the General tab.

4. Click the Tools tab. You see the different tools available for checking your system.

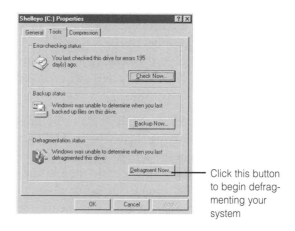

Click this button to begin defrag- menting your system

5. Click the Defragment Now button. The program starts, and you see the progress of the defragmentation.

View the progress of the defragmentation procedure here

You can also start this program from the Start menu. Click Start, Programs, Accessories, System Tools, and then Disk Defragmenter.

Depending on how fragmented your files are, how large your hard disk drive is, and the speed of your PC, the defragmentation process can take anywhere from a few minutes to several hours. Just be patient and let the program do its job. If this is the first time you are defragmenting your hard disk drive, you might want to start it late at night and let it run overnight.

Beyond Survival

Viewing the Defragmenting Progress

If you want to see the results of the defragmenting, you can click the Show Details button. Then click Legend.

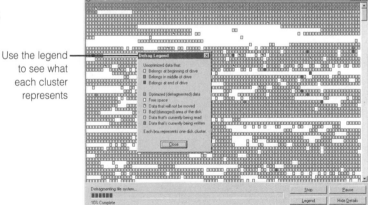

Use the legend to see what each cluster represents

You can watch the progress and see exactly how defragmented your files are (and how they are being fixed).

Cheat Sheet

Cleaning Up Your Disk

1. Double-click the My Computer icon.
2. Right-click the drive you want to clean up and select the Properties command.
3. Click the Disk Cleanup button.
4. Check any additional items to delete. To keep a listed item, uncheck its check box.
5. Click OK.

Setting Other Cleanup Options

1. In the Disk Cleanup dialog box, click the More Options tab.
2. Click the button next to the item you want to remove. If you select Windows components or installed programs, you see the Add/Remove Programs Properties dialog box. You can select which Windows components or programs to remove. (Using the Add/Remove Programs feature is covered in Chapter 9, "Installing and Uninstalling New Programs.") If you select Drive Conversion, you start the Drive Converter Wizard, which leads you through the process of converting the drive.

43

Cleaning Up Files

Another maintenance task you should perform is to clean up files. Windows stores some temporary files—including those in the Recycle Bin, temporary Internet files, Windows uninstall information, and downloaded program files. You can get rid of these files and recover that disk space.

Basic Survival

Cleaning Up Your Disk

If you are worried that something you need will be deleted, don't. Before these files are removed, you see them in a list. You can then select which files are deleted. For instance, I would not delete the uninstall information for Windows, and I would also check your Recycle Bin to make sure it does not contain any files you need.

When you are ready to get rid of files, follow these steps:

1. Double-click the My Computer icon.

2. Right-click the drive you want to clean up and select the Properties command. You see the Properties dialog box showing the General tab.

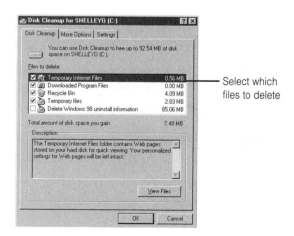

Select which files to delete

3. Click the Disk Cleanup button. You see the DiskCleanup tab, which displays the files selected for deletion. You also see the amount of disk space you will regain if you delete all the selected files.

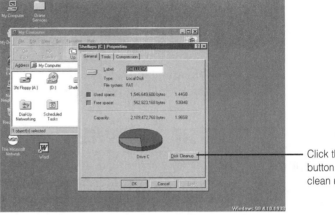

Click this button to clean up

4. Check any additional items to delete. To keep a listed item, uncheck its check box.

5. Click the OK button.

If you want to automatically run this program when you are running out of disk space, click the Settings tab and then check If This Drive Runs Low on Disk Space, Automatically Run Disk Cleanup.

Beyond Survival

Setting Other Cleanup Options

You can do a more thorough "cleaning" by selecting to delete Windows components you don't use, to remove programs, and to convert your disk to FAT32. FAT stands for File Allocation Table, and is the method used to keep track of where files are stored. FAT32 stores files more efficiently, providing more disk space. Also, programs should run faster with FAT32.

To view these options, follow these steps:

1. In the Disk Cleanup dialog box, click the More Options tab.

View the options in this tab ———

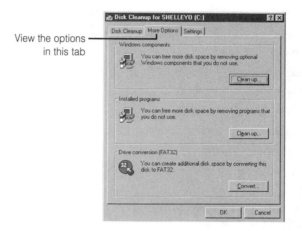

2. Click the button next to the function you want to perform. If you select Windows components or installed programs, you see the Add/Remove Programs Properties dialog box. You can select which Windows components or programs to remove (use the Add/Remove Programs feature covered in Chapter 9, "Installing and Uninstalling New Programs"). If you select Drive Conversion, you start the Drive Converter Wizard, which leads you through the process of converting to FAT32. Follow the onscreen instructions.

Cheat Sheet

Formatting a Floppy Disk

1. Insert the disk you want to format into the drive.
2. Double-click the My Computer icon on the Windows desktop.
3. Right-click your floppy drive (usually drive A) and select the Format command.
4. If necessary, display the Capacity drop-down list and select the correct capacity for your disk.
5. Select the type of format.
6. If you want, enter a label into the Label text box.
7. Click the Start button.
8. When you see a message telling you the format is complete, click OK.

Creating a Startup Disk

1. Exit any programs you have running.
2. Make sure you have a disk and your Windows 98 installation CD handy before you begin.
3. Insert the disk into your A drive.
4. From the Start menu select Programs, Settings, Control Panel to open the Windows 98 Control Panel.
5. Double-click the Add/Remove Programs icon to open the Add/Remove Programs Properties dialog box.
6. Select the Start Disk tab and then select the Create Disk button to begin creating your Start disk.
7. When you are prompted, insert your Windows 98 installation CD in your CD-ROM drive so any files that are needed can be copied to your startup disk.

44

Creating a Startup Disk

Before you can use a floppy disk, you must prepare it for use. This process is called *formatting*. Formatting divides the disk into storage units, where the data will be saved. You may need to format floppy disks. You can also format a disk as a startup disk so that you can use it to start your system in case you can't start from the hard drive.

Note that you should format your hard disk only as a last resort if you are having extreme problems. And before you do so, you may want to consult a data repair expert.

Beyond Survival

Formatting a Floppy Disk

You can purchase preformatted floppy disks to save time. If you did not purchase preformatted disk or you want to format an existing disk, you can do so using Windows. Follow these steps:

1. Insert the disk you want to format into the drive.

2. Double-click the My Computer icon on the Windows desktop.

3. Right-click your floppy drive (usually drive A) and select the Format command. You see the Format dialog box.

Formatting erases all the information on a disk.

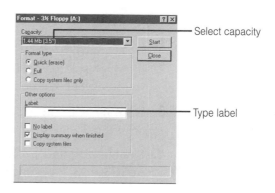

Select capacity

Type label

4. If necessary, display the Capacity drop-down list and select the correct capacity for your disk. You can check the disk box to see the capacity of the disk.

5. Select the type of format. Choosing the Quick option formats the disk and erases all its files; this method doesn't check the disk for bad sectors. Choosing Full erases the files, prepares the disk, and checks for bad sectors. Choosing Copy System Files Only adds the system files to the disk so that you can use this disk to start your PC.

6. If you want, enter a label into the Label text box.

7. Click the Start button.

8. When you see a message telling you the format is complete, click OK.

When the floppy is formatted, you can use it to store files.

Beyond Survival

Creating a Startup Disk

The vast majority of the time, Windows 98 should boot up on your PC without a hitch. But if Windows 98 should ever fail to boot—because of a disk error, because one of the system files becomes damaged or corrupted, or because you accidentally delete one of your system files—you will need a startup disk to boot your PC and access your files.

A startup disk is a bootable disk that contains a copy of the system files used to boot your PC and provide access to peripheral devices like CD-ROM or Zip drives.

Here is the procedure for creating your startup disk:

1. Exit all program you have running.

2. Insert a blank floppy disk into your A drive. Make sure you have your Windows 98 installation CD handy.

3. From the Start menu select Settings, Control Panel to open the Windows 98 Control Panel.

4. Double-click the Add/Remove Programs icon to open the Add/Remove Programs Properties dialog box.

5. Select the Startup Disk tab.

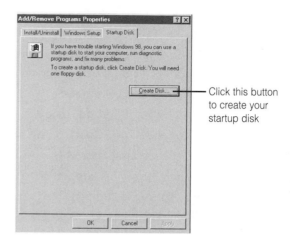

Click this button to create your startup disk

6. Select the Create Disk button to begin creating your startup disk. When prompted, insert your Windows 98 installation CD.

7. When your startup disk is completed, place it in a safe place.

Be sure to keep your startup disk in a safe place until you need it. If you ever make any changes in your PC, such as add new programs to your Startup folder or add/change any peripheral devices, you will need to create a new startup disk to reflect your changes.

Cheat Sheet

Backing Up All Files

1. From the Start menu select Programs, Accessories, System Tools, and then select Backup.
2. Select Create a New Backup Job and click OK.
3. Select Back Up My Computer.
4. Select All Selected Files and click Next.
5. Select the device you are backing up to.
6. Select what backup options you want turned on and click Next.
7. Type a name for the backup job and click Start.
8. When the backup is complete, exit the program by clicking its Close (×) button.

Backing Up Selected Files

1. From the Start menu select Programs, Accessories, System Tools, and then Backup.
2. Select Back Up Selected Files, Folders, and Drives; then click Next.
3. Select the files you want to back up by selecting the check box in front of either a file or a folder. You can expand the drive and folder list by clicking the plus sign next to a particular drive or folder.
4. After you have selected all the files you want to back up, click Next.
5. Select All Selected Files and click Next.
6. Select the device you are backing up to.
7. Select what backup options you want turned on and click Next.
8. Type a name for the backup job and click Start.
9. When the backup is complete, exit the Backup program by clicking its Close (×) button.

45

Backing Up Your System

The best insurance against any potential problems to your PC is a recent backup of your important files. Windows 98 comes with a backup utility program you can use to back up selected files or your entire hard disk drive.

Basic Survival

**Backing Up
All Files**

You can use the Backup utility in Windows 98 to selectively back up any files or groups of files on your hard disk drive. In most cases when you back up files, you will be doing your backup to one or more floppy disks or to a slightly larger storage medium such as a Zip drive. At first you might want to make a complete backup set. Then you can back up just selected files.

Here's how you can use the Windows 98 Backup utility to back up all files to a floppy disk:

1. From the Start menu select Programs, Accessories, System Tools, and then Backup to start the Windows 98 Backup utility program.

2. Select Create a New Backup Job and click OK.

3. Select Back Up My Computer.

Click this option button to back up all files and folders on your local drive

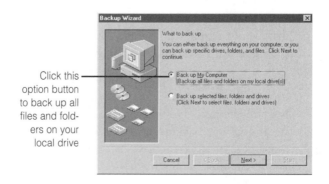

4. Select All Selected Files and click Next.

5. Select the device you are backing up to. If you are backing up to a floppy disk in your A drive, select Drive A.

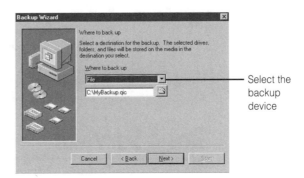

Select the backup device

6. Select what backup options you want turned on and click Next.

7. Type a name for the backup job and click Start. Backup will prompt you to enter a second and a third disk, or as many disks as you need to complete your backup.

8. When the backup is complete, exit the Backup program by clicking its Close (×) button.

Beyond Survival

Speeding Up the Backup Process

Backing up your entire hard disk drive to floppy disks can easily seem like an endless exercise in futility—especially because the hard disk drives in most PCs these days are in the 2–3GB (gigabyte) range. To back up a 2GB drive onto 1.44MB floppy disk would require more than 1300 disks and a lot more time than you want to spend swapping floppies.

If you want to back up your entire hard disk drive, you can still use the Backup utility but you will need a storage medium that is up to the task. This means you will need to use some type of streaming tape backup device or one of the large capacity removable media type drives such as the Iomega Jaz drive or the Syquest removable media drive. If you have to do a lot of backups, consider adding one of these drives to your system.

The Backup utility includes options specifically for use with tape drives such as

- The capability to automatically detect a tape drive

- An option to erase or format a tape in a tape drive

- An option to perform a file verification on the tape contents after the backup

- An option to perform full or incremental backups

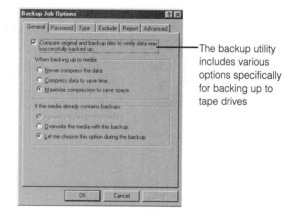

The backup utility includes various options specifically for backing up to tape drives

Backing Up Selected Files

Even though the Windows 98 Backup utility will allow you to perform incremental backups, there are several good reasons not to. In theory incremental backups sound like a good idea—you first perform a full backup, and then the next few times you perform your backup, you only back up files that have changed. Sounds like a good idea until you have to restore just a few files. If your incremental backups are spread across several tapes, you may have trouble locating the particular tape that stores the file or files you are looking for. My advice is to perform a full backup on one tape and let your backups run overnight.

As another alternative, you can simply back up selected files—for instance, all files in a particular folder. Follow these steps to back up just selected files:

1. From the Start menu select Programs, Accessories, System Tools, and then select Backup to start the Windows 98 backup utility program.

2. Select Back Up Selected Files, folders, and Drives. Then click Next.

3. Select the files you want to back up by selecting the check box in front of either a file or folder. You can expand the drive and folder list by clicking the plus sign next to a particular drive or folder.

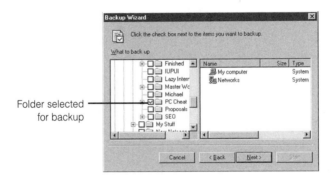

Folder selected
for backup

4. After you have selected all the files you want to back up, click Next.

5. Select All Selected Files and click Next.

6. Select the device you are backing up to. If you are backing up to a floppy disk in your A drive, select Drive A.

7. Select what backup options you want turned on and click Next.

8. Type a name for the backup job and click Start.

   Backup will prompt you to enter a second and a third disk, or as many disks as you need to complete your backup. You see a message when the backup is complete.

9. Exit the Backup program by clicking its Close (×) button.

Cheat Sheet

Restoring Files

1. From the Start menu select Programs, Accessories, System Tools, and then select Backup to start the Windows 98 backup utility program.

2. Select Restore Backed Up Files and click OK.

3. Select your restore device, which is the device you backed up your files to. If you backed up to a floppy disk, make sure you load the disk (or if you backed up to more than one disk, load the first disk) into your drive.

4. Select your backup set on your backup device. Click Next to continue.

5. If you aren't restoring the entire backup, select the file or files you want to restore. Click Next.

6. Select where you want you want to restore the files to (usually the Original Location).

7. Select how the files are restored—that is, how files that exist on the original drive and in the backup set should be handled.

8. Click the Start button. When the restore is complete, you see a message box. Click OK, and then exit the Backup program.

46

Restoring a Backup

In the last chapter, you learned how to perform backups using the Windows 98 Backup utility. You learned to back up to floppy disks (when you are only backing up a few files) and to tape (when you need to back up your entire hard disk drive). Well, backups are no good if you can't restore the files you backed up, so in this chapter you will see what you need to do to restore backed up files.

Basic Survival

Restoring Files

As you might expect, the restore process is the opposite of the backup procedure. That is, the files are copied from the backup media (disks or tapes) to your hard disk. Here's how to restore the files you just backed up:

1. From the Start menu select Programs, Accessories, System Tools, and then select Backup to start the Windows 98 backup utility program.

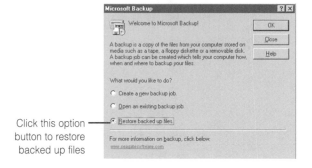

Click this option button to restore backed up files

2. Select Restore Backed Up Files and click OK.

3. Select your restore device, which is the device you backed up your files to. If you backed up to a floppy disk make sure you load the disk (or if you backed up to more than one disk, load the first disk) into your drive.

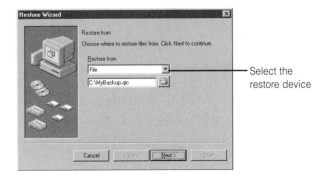

Select the restore device

4. Select your backup set on your backup device. Click Next to continue.

5. If you aren't restoring the entire backup set (that is, all the files in the backup set), select the file or files you want to restore.

6. Select the backup set you want to restore and click OK.

Select the backup set you want to restore

7. Select the items you want to restore and click Next.

Click the check box next to the items you want to restore

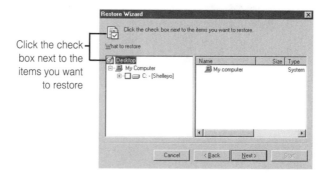

8. Select where you want you want to restore the files to (usually the original location).

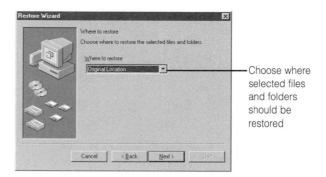

Choose where selected files and folders should be restored

9. Select how the files are restored—that is, how files that exist on the original drive and in the backup set should be handled.

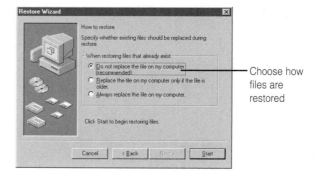

Choose how files are restored

10. Click the Start button. When the restore is complete, you see a message box. Click OK. Then exit the Backup program.

Cheat Sheet

Installing a New Printer

1. Click the Start button, select Settings, and then select Printers.
2. Double-click the Add Printer icon.
3. Click the Next button to continue with the installation.
4. Select the Manufacturers name from the list. Then select the printer's name. Click Next.
5. Select the appropriate port and click Next.
6. Enter a name for the printer, or accept the one Windows has given it.
7. Select whether you want the new printer to be the default printer. Then click the Next button.
8. Select whether you want to print a test page. If so, Windows prints a test page, and you are asked whether it printed successfully. Click Yes.
9. Click Finish.

Handling Print Jobs

1. Click the Start button, select Settings, and then select Printers.
2. Double-click the printer you want to view.
3. To pause a print job, open the Printer menu and select Pause Printing. To restart, open the Printer menu and uncheck Pause Printing.
4. To cancel a print job, select the job you want to cancel. Then open the Document menu and select Cancel Printing.
5. To close the printer window, click its Close (×) button.

47

Setting Up Your Printer

If you purchase a new printer or add a printer, you need to set it up. Windows includes a wizard that leads you step by step through the process. You can also use the Printer Control Panel to change printer options.

The print queue lists the documents that you have sent to a printer, and it shows how far along the printing is. Using the print queue, you can pause, restart, or cancel print jobs.

Basic Survival

Installing a New Printer

You can add a new printer to your Windows setup using a step-by-step guide called a wizard. Use the wizard any time you get a new printer or change printers.

Follow these steps to set up a new printer:

1. Click the Start button, select Settings, and then select Printers. You see the Printers folder.

2. Double-click the Add Printer icon. You see the opening of the wizard.

3. Click the Next button to continue with the installation.

4. Select the Manufacturers name from the list. Then select the printer's name. Click Next.

Select manufacturer ——— 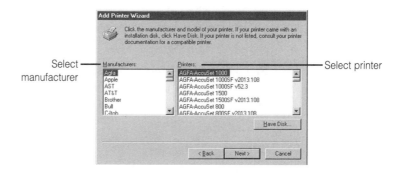 ——— Select printer

5. Select the appropriate port (the one your printer is connected to) and click Next. Most printers are connected via the LPT1 port.

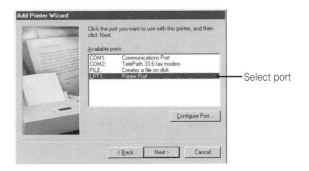

Select port

6. Enter a name for the printer, or accept the one Windows has given it.

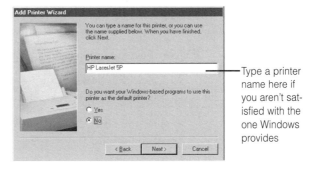

Type a printer name here if you aren't satisfied with the one Windows provides

7. Select whether you want the new printer to be the default printer. Then click Next.

Click the Back button to go back a step.

8. Select whether you want to print a test page. If so, Windows prints a test page, and you are asked whether it printed successfully. Click Yes.

9. Click the Finish button. Windows then adds the new printer's icon to the Printers folder.

Handling Print Jobs

While the printer is printing, you see the printer icon in the status bar. If needed, you can view the print queue to see which jobs are printing and to check the status of a print job. For short documents, you may not have time to see the queue; the data is sent to the printer and processed too quickly. For longer jobs or multiple jobs, however, you can view the print queue and make changes, if needed.

For instance, you may want to pause printing when you have a change to make in the text or when you want to load a different paper type. If you discover an error in the job you are printing or if you decide you need to add something before printing the job, you can cancel the print job.

Follow these steps to display the print queue:

As a shortcut, you can double-click the printer icon in the taskbar to display the print queue.

1. Click the Start button, select Settings, and then select Printers. You see the Printers folder.

2. Double-click the printer you want to view. The Printer window displays a list of the documents in the queue plus statistics about the documents being printed.

Current job ——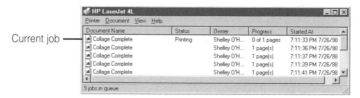

If the print queue window is empty, there is nothing in the print queue.

3. To pause a print job, open the Printer menu and select Pause Printing. To restart, open the Printer menu and uncheck Pause Printing.

4. To cancel a print job, select the job you want to cancel. Then open the Document menu and select Cancel Printing.

5. To close the printer window, click its Close (×) button.

Beyond Survival

Setting the Default Printer

If you have more than one printer connected, you must select one as the default. The default printer is the printer your applications automatically use when you choose to print. (You can always change the printer used for an individual job in an application.) Follow these steps to select a default printer:

1. Click the Start button, select Settings, and then select Printers. You see the Printers folder.

2. Select the printer you want to choose as the default.

3. Open the File menu and select Set as Default.

Cheat Sheet

Running the Hardware Wizard

1. From the Start menu select Settings, Control Panel to open the Windows Control Panel.

2. In the Control Panel, double-click the Add New Hardware icon to start the Add New Hardware Wizard.

3. Click Next twice to start the wizard.

4. In most cases the wizard should be able to locate the device on its own. But if it cannot locate the new device, you will need to help. Follow the prompts supplied by the wizard. Try to let the wizard do as much of the search process as it can. If the wizard still cannot locate the new device, select the new device (when prompted) from the list of devices Windows knows how to configure.

5. After the new device has been identified to Windows, the wizard should have no trouble configuring the device. Make sure you have your Windows or printer CD handy in case the wizard prompts you to load it so it can retrieve a device driver.

48

Installing New Hardware

Installing new hardware in your PC has never been easier. Years ago, when you wanted to add a device like a sound card or an internal modem, you had to worry about making sure all the hardware interrupt and memory settings were correct and not being used by an existing device, and whether you had the right hardware device driver installed. Experienced users sometimes took hours to install a new device and inexperienced users simply gave up in disgust or paid someone to install the peripheral device.

Windows 98 includes a feature called *Plug and Play*, which makes installing new hardware devices practically as simple as turning on your PC. The Plug and Play feature in Windows 98 (and 95, as well) works with Plug and Play hardware devices and will automatically detect what settings are needed by the device and make all the configuration changes for you. Windows 98 Plug and Play will also prompt you to insert your Windows 98 installation CD, download, and install the proper hardware device driver if one is needed.

Basic Survival

Plug and Play Setup

In most cases, when you install a new hardware device in your PC, Windows 98 will detect the new device when you boot your computer and begin configuring the device for you. During this configuration, Windows 98 will make sure that the settings it uses for the new device don't conflict with settings on existing hardware devices in your PC. If the new hardware device requires a device driver, Windows will prompt you to put your installation CD into your CD-ROM drive and attempt to locate and install the proper device driver.

Follow these steps:

1. After installing the new device, restart your computer.

2. When Windows detects the device and prompts you for information, follow the steps to set up the new device.

Beyond Survival

Running the Hardware Wizard

As good as Plug and Play may sound on paper, it isn't perfect; occasionally, some devices will not be configured properly, Windows will be unable to properly identify the device, or Windows will be unable to locate the proper device driver for the new peripheral. When this happens, you will need to run the Add New Hardware Wizard to help jump-start the installation and configuration process.

To run the Add New Hardware Wizard, follow these steps:

1. From the Start menu select Settings, Control Panel to open the windows Control Panel.

2. In the Control Panel, double-click the Add New Hardware icon to start the Add New Hardware Wizard.

3. Click the Next button twice to start the wizard. The wizard will begin by searching for the new hardware device you have installed.

4. In most cases the wizard should be able to locate the device on its own, but if it cannot, you will need to help. Follow the prompts supplied by the wizard. Try to let the wizard do as much of the search process as it can. If the wizard still cannot locate the new device, select the new device (when prompted) from the list of devices Windows knows how to configure.

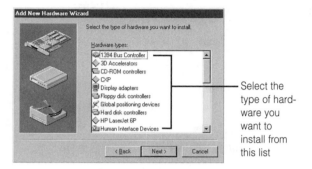

Select the type of hardware you want to install from this list

5. After the new device has been identified to Windows, the wizard should have no trouble configuring the device. Make sure you have your installation CD handy in case the wizard prompts you to load it so it can retrieve a device driver.

Cheat Sheet

Adding a Task

1. Click Start and then select Programs, Accessories, System Tools.
2. Select Scheduled Tasks.
3. Double-click Add Scheduled Task.
4. Click Next.
5. Select the program to run and click Next.
6. Type a name and then select when you want to perform the task: daily, weekly, monthly, one time only, when your computer starts, or when you log on. Click the Next button.
7. Make any other selections and click Next.
8. Click the Finish button.

Deleting a Scheduled Task

1. Click Start and then select Programs, Accessories, System Tools.
2. Select Scheduled Tasks.
3. Right-click the program you want to delete and click Delete.
4. Click Yes to confirm the deletion.
5. Close the Scheduled Tasks list by clicking its Close (×) button.

Modifying a Scheduled Task

1. Click Start and then select Programs, Accessories, System Tools.
2. Select Scheduled Tasks.
3. Right-click the program you want to modify and then select Properties.
4. On the Task tab, make any changes to the program you want to run.
5. Click the Schedule tab and then make any changes to when the program runs.
6. Click the Settings tab and make any changes to what happens after the task is completed and during idle time.
7. Click OK.
8. Close the Scheduled Tasks list by clicking its Close (×) button.

49

Scheduling Tasks

Sometimes it is hard to remember when you last performed a task. Also, it might be more convenient to schedule some tasks during the night, when you aren't using your computer. You can use the Scheduled Task Wizard to schedule maintenance tasks, such as running backups or checking your email. You can run any program on your system.

Basic Survival

Adding a Task

To set up a scheduled task, you can run the Scheduled Task Wizard. This wizard leads you step-by-step through the process of selecting the program to run, when you want to run the program, how often, and so on. Follow these steps:

1. Choose Start, Programs, Accessories, System Tools.

2. Select Scheduled Tasks. You see the list of Scheduled Tasks.

3. Double-click Add Scheduled Task. You see the first step of the Scheduled Task Wizard, which gives you an overview of the process.

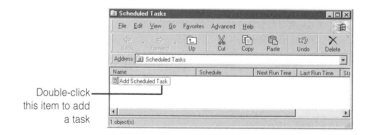

Double-click this item to add a task

4. Click Next. You are prompted to select the program you want to run.

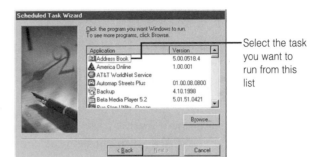

Select the task you want to run from this list

5. Select the program to run and click Next. You are prompted to type a name for the task as well as select when to perform the task.

Specify the name of the task, as well as how often you want it to be performed

6. Type a name and then select when you want to perform the task: daily, weekly, monthly, one time only, when your computer starts, or when you log on. Click the Next button.

Depending on what you selected for when to run the program, you see different options for that task. For instance, if you select Daily, you select the start time, what days to perform, and the start date.

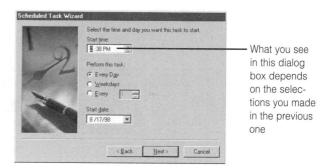

What you see in this dialog box depends on the selections you made in the previous one

7. Make any other selections and click Next. You see the final dialog box.

8. Click the Finish button.

The program will run at the time and interval you selected.

Deleting a Scheduled Task

If you add a task and change your mind, you can unschedule it by deleting it from the Scheduled Tasks list. Follow these steps:

1. Click Start and then select Programs, Accessories, System Tools.

2. Select Scheduled Tasks. You see the list of Scheduled Tasks.

3. Right-click the program you want to delete and click Delete.

4. Click Yes to confirm the deletion.

5. Close the Scheduled Tasks list by clicking its Close (×) button.

Beyond Survival

Modifying a Scheduled Task

If you add a task and find that you don't like the schedule you selected or if want to set other options, you can make a change. To do so, display the task list. Follow these steps:

1. Click Start and then select Programs, Accessories, System Tools.

2. Select Scheduled Tasks. You see the list of Scheduled Tasks.

List of scheduled tasks

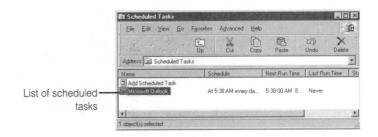

3. Right-click the program you want to modify and then select Properties. You see the Properties dialog box.

4. On the Task tab, make any changes to the program you want to run.

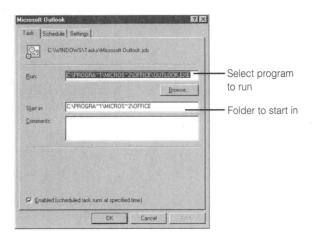

Select program to run

Folder to start in

5. Click the Schedule tab and then make any changes to when the program runs.

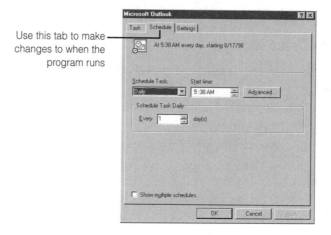

Use this tab to make changes to when the program runs

6. Click the Settings tab and make any changes to what happens after the task is completed and during idle time.

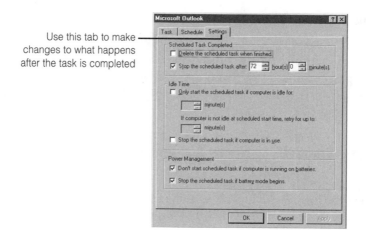

Use this tab to make changes to what happens after the task is completed

7. Click OK.

8. Close the Scheduled Tasks list by clicking its Close (×) button.

Cheat Sheet

Running the Device Manager

1. From the Start menu select Settings, Control Panel to open the Windows Control Panel.
2. In the Control Panel, double-click the System icon to open the System Properties dialog box.
3. Select the Device Manager tab to access the Device Manager.
4. In the Device Manager, a red × on a hardware item means that device has been disabled. A yellow exclamation mark means there is a problem with the device. To see how Device Manager is attempting to diagnose the problem, select the device and then select the Properties button. Follow any suggested fixes.

Common-Sense Tips for Protecting Your PC From Viruses

- Install an anti-virus program and make sure you regularly update the virus definition files.
- Scan all disks before you copy any files from them onto your PC.
- Write-protect all program disks before installing the program to prevent possible infections. If you have a choice, purchase programs on CDs rather than disks since CDs cannot be "accidentally" infected.
- Never start or boot your PC with a disk in the drive.

Scanning for Viruses Using Norton Anti-Virus

1. Exit all programs you have running.
2. Open the Start menu and select Programs, Norton Anti-Virus, and then select the Norton Anti-Virus icon to start the program.
3. Select the drive you want to scan by selecting the corresponding check box.
4. Select the Scan Now button to begin your scan.

Troubleshooting Problems

Windows 98 doesn't give you very much in the way of tools to help you diagnose problems with your PC. There is one tool, however, that will provide some rudimentary information on some minor problems with your PC: the Device Manager. You can also purchase other system maintenance programs, including a program for scanning for viruses.

Basic Survival

Running the Device Manager

Although the Device Manager is definitely not in the class of "heavy-duty" diagnostic tools, you can use it to spot some simple problems in your PC such as memory or interrupt conflicts with peripheral devices, or when a device driver is not installed or functioning properly.

To use the Device Manager, follow these steps:

1. From the Start menu select Settings, Control Panel to open the Windows Control Panel.

2. In the Control Panel, double-click the System icon to open the System Properties dialog box.

3. Select the Device Manager tab to access the Device Manager.

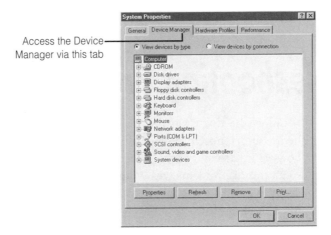

Access the Device
Manager via this tab

4. In the Device Manager, a red × on a hardware item means that device has been disabled. A yellow exclamation mark means there is a problem with the device. To see how Device Manager is attempting to diagnose the problem, select the device and then select the Properties button.

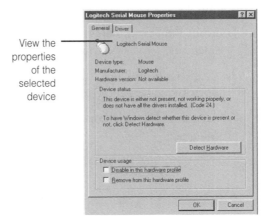

View the
properties
of the
selected
device

5. Try the suggested changes listed in the dialog box.

Beyond Survival

Avoiding Viruses

Just as viral infections can severely debilitate you, computer viruses can wreak havoc with your PC. Computer viruses, though not biological in nature, can nonetheless be just as destructive as their biological namesakes. Computer viruses can run the gamut from mildly annoying to totally wiping out your programs and data. They mimic the behavior of biological viruses by infecting the host computer, spreading from computer to computer, and eventually causing destruction.

The most common method of transmittal is via a floppy disk infected with a virus, but your computer can also become infected from files you download from bulletin board services (BBSs) and from the Internet. It can also become infected from files attached to email messages you receive.

To protect your PC from computer viruses, you need to purchase an anti-virus program and use it to scan your PC's hard disk drive. If your PC is infected with a virus, you can use the anti-virus program to remove the virus.

Nonetheless, your first priority should be prevention. Here are a few suggestions for avoiding viruses:

- Make sure you have an anti-virus program installed and running on your PC

- Make sure your regularly (preferably every month or two) update the virus definitions in your anti-virus program

- Make sure you scan every floppy disk and email you receive before using or reading them

- Never turn on or start your PC with a floppy disk in your A drive that you've never scanned

Scanning Your PC With an Anti-Virus Program

There are several companies that produce PC anti-virus programs. Two of the best known are Symantec (www.symantec.com) and McAfee (www.mcafee.com). Both do an exceptional job of scanning your PC for viruses and removing any viruses that might be found, and both provide monthly virus definition updates to help you fight new viruses as they are produced.

If you select Norton Anti-Virus from Symantec, here is what you need to do to use the program to scan your PC for viruses:

1. From the Start menu select Programs, Norton Anti-Virus, and then select the Norton Anti-Virus icon to start the program.

2. Make sure all drives you want to scan are checked in the Drives list.

Check the drives you want to scan

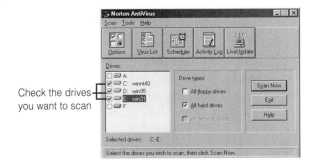

3. Select the Scan Now button to begin scanning the designated drives.

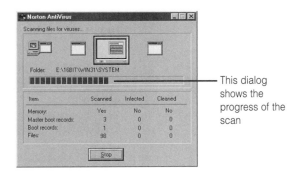

This dialog shows the progress of the scan

4. If the program detects a virus infecting your drive, it will present a warning message and several options for eradicating the virus.

Just as you can manually scan your PC's hard disk drives, you can also manually scan any floppy disks you acquire by simply selecting drive A instead of your hard disk drives.

Regardless of which anti-virus program you install, you should regularly scan your PC for viruses and most importantly, make sure you regularly update your anti-viral definition files by downloading the updated files from the program's manufacturer.

Connecting to the Internet

You are no longer limited to just your office or home PC. With your PC and the right equipment, you can connect to the Internet, a network of networks. Once connected, you gain access to a wealth of information and services. If you have a modem and an Internet connection, read this part to see some of the things you can do. The following topics are covered:

- Getting Connected to the Internet

- Starting and Exiting Internet Explorer

- Browsing the Internet

- Searching the Internet

- Sending and Receiving Email

- Joining Newsgroups

Cheat Sheet

Setting Up for the Internet

1. Choose Start, Programs, Internet Explorer, Connection Wizard.
2. Click the Next button.
3. If you have an Internet account, click I Want to Set Up a New Connection on This Computer to My Existing Internet Account Using My Phone Line or Local Area Network (LAN), and then click Next.
4. Specify how you want to connect and then click Next.
5. Choose whether to use an existing dial-up connection or to create a new one, and then click Next.
6. Type the telephone number you use to connect to your ISP and click Next.
7. Type your username and the password assigned to you by your ISP, and then click Next.
8. If you don't want to change the advanced settings, click No and then click Next.
9. Type a name for your dial-up connection and then click Next.
10. Select Yes if you want to set up your Internet mail account, and then click Next.
11. Specify whether you want to use an existing account or to create a new account and then click Next.
12. To create a new account, follow the prompts.
13. Select Yes if you want to set up a new account and then click Next.
14. Specify whether you want to use an existing account or create a new account, and then click Next.
15. To create a new account, follow the prompts.
16. Select No when prompted to set up an Internet directory service account, and then click Next.
17. Click the Finish button to complete the setup.

Getting Connected to the Internet

To connect to the Internet, you need to have a modem, a phone line (or network connection), and an Internet service provider. You also need a browser, which enables you to view content and also usually provides mail and newsgroup features. With all this equipment, you can get set up.

Basic Survival

What You Need To Get Connected

The first thing you need to get connected is a modem. Modem stands for *mo*dulator-*dem*odulator, which means it translates the PC's digital information to analog information that the phone line can carry, and sends the analog information over the phone lines. The receiving modem then translates the analog information back to digital.

You also need a phone line. You can use your existing phone, but then you have to coordinate when the line is used for the PC and when the line is used for phone calls. You may want to install a second line specifically for your modem. Alternatively, you may connect through your company's network rather than through the phone lines.

In addition to the hardware, you need an Internet service provider (ISP). This company provides you with a hookup to its network. From your ISP's network, you can get connected to the Internet. The ISP also provides the necessary programs to browse the Internet, handle email, and read newsgroup messages.

Try the Web site www.thelist. com for a list of ISPs.

One easy way to get connected to the Internet is through an online service like America Online. You can take advantage of all the features of the online service in addition to using it as a gateway to the Internet. You can also find an independent service provider that focuses just on Internet connections. These may provide additional features, such as helping you publish your own Web page. You can find independent service providers by looking in the Yellow Pages, by asking friends and coworkers for recommendations, or by checking out one of the many Internet directories or magazines for information.

For each task you do on the Internet, you need a program for handling that particular task. For instance, to browse the World Wide Web, you need a Web browser. To read and send email messages, you need an email program. To participate in newsgroups, you need a newsreader.

Usually your Internet service provider provides the necessary software. You can also use two popular programs—Netscape Communicator and Internet Explorer—to access the Internet. Both programs are really a complete suite of Internet tools and include all the programs you need to browse, send mail, transfer files, join newsgroups, and so on.

Setting Up for the Internet

After you have all the equipment and connections, you need to get set up. Windows makes it easy to set up by providing a Connection Wizard. The following steps lead you through the entire wizard, including setting up a new Internet account, mail account, and newsgroup account. If you already have an account, select that option and follow the onscreen instructions. If you don't want to set up a particular account, you can skip it. You can run the wizard again to set up the accounts you didn't set up the first time.

The following steps give you the basic procedure, but if you make different choices, the steps may vary. Simply follow the wizard's instructions.

Follow these steps to set up for the Internet for the first time:

1. Choose Start, Programs, Internet Explorer, and click Connection Wizard.

2. If you don't already have an Internet provider and want to find one and set up an account, select this option and then click Next. Follow the wizard's directions.

If you have an existing account and want to set up your PC for this account, select this option and then click Next. (These steps cover how to set up the PC for an existing account.)

Click the option
button that best
describes your
situation

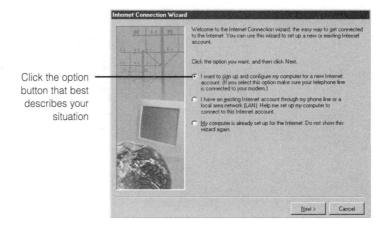

3. Specify how you are connected—through an Internet service provider or LAN or through an online service. Click Next.

Specify whether
you plan to connect
to the Internet via
an ISP or an online
service provider

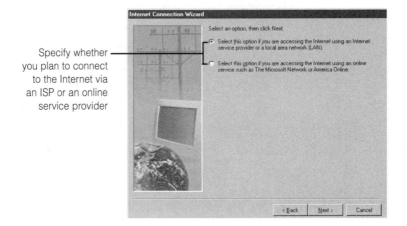

275

Click the Back button to go back through your choices and make a change.

4. Select how to you get connected—through the phone line or LAN. For information on networks (LANs), see Part VII of this book. Click Next.

5. Select the modem you want to use and click Next.

6. Choose whether to use an existing dial-up connection or create a new one and then click Next. If you have already set up a connection, select Existing. If you have never set up your PC for an Internet connection, select New.

Decide whether you want to use an existing dial-up connection or to create a new one

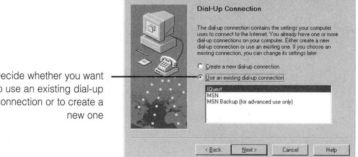

7. If you choose to create a new dial-up connection, type the telephone number you use to connect to your Internet service provider and click Next.

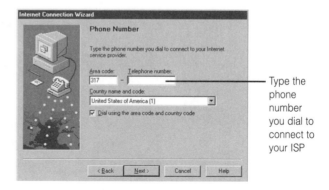

Type the phone number you dial to connect to your ISP

8. Type your username and the password assigned to you by your ISP, and then click Next.

276

9. If you don't want to change the advanced settings, click No and then click Next.

10. Type a name for your dial-up connection—any name you want—and then click Next.

11. Select Yes if you want to set up your Internet mail account, and then click Next.

12. If you chose to set up a mail account, specify whether you want to use an existing account or create a new account and then click Next. If you have already set up a mail account, select existing and then select that account. If you are brand new to the Internet and have not set up an account, select New.

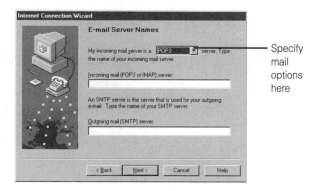

Specify mail options here

13. To create a new account, type the name you want displayed in messages and then click Next.

14. Type the email address assigned to you by your ISP, and then click Next.

15. Enter the requested information about your incoming and outgoing mail servers (you can get this information from your ISP), and then click Next.

16. Specify logon instructions, and then click Next.

17. Type a name for the mail account, and then click Next.

18. Select Yes if you want to set up a news account and then click Next.

19. Specify whether you want to use an existing account or create a new account, and then click Next.

20. If you chose to create a new account, type the name you want displayed in messages posted to the newsgroup, and then click Next.

21. Type the email address assigned to you by your ISP, and then click Next.

22. Enter the requested information about your news server and then click Next. (Your ISP should provide this information.)

Type the name of your Internet news server here

23. Type a name to identify the news account, and then click Next.

24. Select No when prompted to set up an Internet directory service account, and then click Next.

25. Click the Finish button to complete the setup.

Beyond Survival

Making Changes to the Setup

If you need to make a change—for instance, suppose that you didn't set up a certain account—you can rerun the Internet Connection Wizard. Follow these steps:

1. Choose Start, Programs, Internet Explorer, and click Connection Wizard.

2. Make the appropriate selections to change the account (or set up a new one).

Cheat Sheet

Logging On to the Internet

1. Double-click the Internet icon.
2. When prompted, sign on to your Internet provider.

Logging Off from the Internet

1. To exit the browser, click the Close button in the upper-right corner of the browser window.
2. Right-click on the Internet connection icon in the status bar and choose Disconnect to end your ISP connection.

52

Starting and Exiting Internet Explorer

After you have your Internet connection set up, you can start Internet Explorer and browse the Internet. If you have problems connecting—the line is busy, for instance—try again. If you continue to have problems, check with your ISP.

Basic Survival

Logging On

Your Internet provider will give you specific instructions for how to log on to the Internet. Here are the basic steps:

1. Double-click the Internet icon. Usually the installation program sets up an icon for Internet access.

2. When prompted, sign on to your Internet provider. Usually you type your username and password and then click Connect.

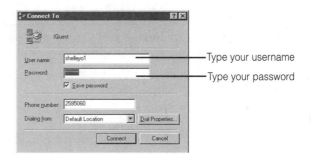

Type your username
Type your password

When you connect, you see your start page (sometimes called a "home page"), which will vary depending on which browser you are using. The following shows the default start page for people using Internet Explorer—home.microsoft.com.

This is the default
start page for
Internet Explorer

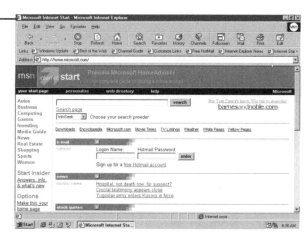

Logging Off

When you are finished browsing the Internet, you need to exit Internet Explorer and also end your connection to your Internet provider. Follow these steps:

1. To exit the browser, click the Close button in the upper-right corner of the browser window.

2. Right-click the Internet connection icon in the status bar and choose Disconnect to end your ISP connection.

Beyond Survival

Changing Your Connection Settings

You may need to make changes to your connection settings. For instance, the number you dial to connect to your ISP may change. Follow these steps to review and make any changes to your connection:

1. Double-click the My Computer icon.

2. Double-click the Dial-Up Networking folder.

3. Right-click the connection you want to change and then select Properties. You see the Properties dialog box for your connection.

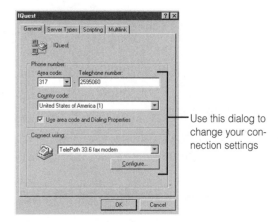

Use this dialog to change your connection settings

4. Make any changes and click OK.

Cheat Sheet

Using Links to Explore the Internet

1. Click the link on the Web page.
2. Continue clicking links until you find the information you want.

Typing an Address

1. Click in the Address text box.
2. Type the address you want to go to and press Enter.

Adding a Site to Your Favorites List

1. Go to the page you want to add.
2. Open the Favorites menu and select the Add To Favorites command.
3. Type a name for the page and then click OK.

Going to a Site in Your Favorites List

1. Click the Favorites button on the toolbar.
2. Click the site you want to visit.

Using the History List

1. Click the History button in the toolbar.
2. If necessary, select the week whose list you want to review.
3. Click the site you want.

53

Browsing the Internet

Everything on the Web is displayed as a document page, and a Web page can contain text, graphics, sounds, movies, and links to other Web pages. These links are what make it possible to browse the Web. When you click a link, you're taken to another page on the Web, which contains information as well as other links. Not only can you review the information and pictures on each page, but you can also click any of the links to get additional information.

This chapter describes how to browse the Internet by using links, by typing an address, and by clicking the toolbar buttons.

Basic Survival

Clicking Links To Browse

Information on the Internet is easy to browse because documents contain links to other pages, documents, and sites. Simply click a link to view the associated page. A link may take you to another page in that document, to another document at that site, or to an entirely new site. The journey is half the fun! Links usually appear underlined; images also may be links. You can tell whether an image (or text) is a link by placing your mouse pointer on it; if the pointer changes into a pointing hand, the image (or text) is a link.

Pointer looks like a hand when over a link

If you see an error message when you click a link, it could indicate that the link isn't accurate or that the server is too busy. Try again.

To navigate from page to page using a link, follow these steps:

1. From any Web page, click the link. For instance, you can click any of the links on the Amazon.com page (an online bookstore) shown in the following figure.

Links

2. Continue clicking links until you find the information you want.

Typing an Address

Each Web page has a unique address called a *URL*, which stands for Uniform Resource Locator. For example, here's the address for the White House:

```
http://www.whitehouse.gov
```

The first part is the protocol (usually http:// for Web pages). Next you have the domain name (whitehouse) and then the extension (usually .com, .net, .gov, .edu, or .mil), which indicates the type of site (commercial, network resources, government, educational, or military, respectively). You can find addresses in advertisements, articles, books, and so on.

Typing a site's address is the fastest way to get to that site. Follow these steps:

1. Click in the Address text box. The entire address should be highlighted.

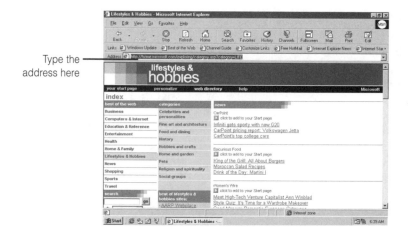

Type the
address here

2. Type the address you want to go to and press Enter. You see that page.

Using Toolbar Buttons

When you click a link or type an address, you journey from page to page. To help you navigate among the pages, you can also use the buttons in the toolbar. You can go back to pages you have previously viewed, forward through pages after going back, and back to your start page. Do any of the following:

- Click the Back button to go back to a page you previously viewed.

- If you have gone back, you can also go forward. Click the Forward button to move forward through the pages you've already visited.

- To return to your start page, click the Home button in the toolbar.

Beyond Survival

Adding a Site to Your Favorites List

When you find a site that you especially like, you might want a quick way to return to it without having to browse from link to link or having to remember the address. You can add the page to a list of favorite sites.

287

Internet Explorer uses the term Favorites and displays the items in folders. If you use another browser, you may follow a different procedure. For instance, Netscape Navigator uses bookmarks.

To add a site to your Favorites list, follow these steps:

1. Go to the page you want to add.

2. Open the Favorites menu and select Add To Favorites.

3. Type a name for the page and then click OK.

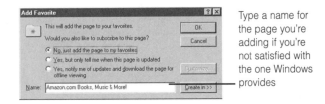

Type a name for the page you're adding if you're not satisfied with the one Windows provides

Going to a Site in Your Favorites List

After you have added a site to your Favorites list, you can easily reach that site by displaying the list and selecting the site. Follow these steps to go to a site in Internet Explorer:

1. Click the Favorites button on the toolbar. The pane on the left side of the screen contains your Favorites list, and the right pane contains the current page.

Your list of favorites (these favorites have been organized into folders)

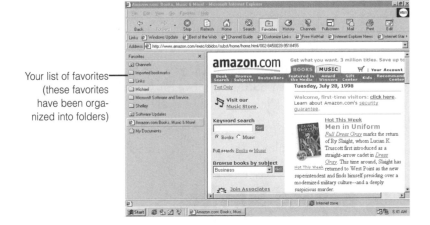

2. Click the site you want to visit. You see that page.

3. To close the Favorites bar, click its Close (×) button.

You can organize your list into folders (as shown in this example). To do so, use the Favorites, Organize Favorites command.

Using the History List

As you browse from link to link, you might remember a site that you liked, but not remember that site's name or address. You can easily return to sites you have visited. In both Internet Explorer and Navigator, you display the History list, but the procedure is a little different for Navigator.

To view a history list in Internet Explorer, follow these steps:

1. Click the History button in the toolbar. You see the History list in a pane on the left side of the window.

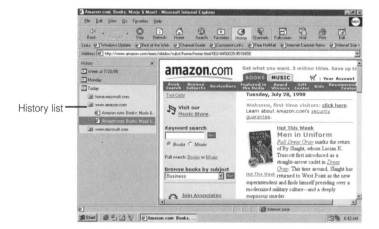

History list

2. If necessary, select the week whose list you want to review.

3. Click the site you want. Internet Explorer displays that site.

4. To close the History Bar, click its Close (×) button.

Cheat Sheet

Searching the Internet

1. Click the Search button in your browser's toolbar.
2. Select the search engine you want to use.
3. In the text box, type the word or phrase you want to find.
4. Click the Search button.
5. To go to any of the found sites, click the link to that site.

54

Searching the Internet

Browsing around is time-consuming (but fun). You never know where you'll end up. You might start out researching a legitimate project and end up checking out pictures of bulldogs on the bulldog page. When you have an idea of what you want to find and want to see what's available, you can search the Internet.

Basic Survival

To search the Internet, you use a search engine—there are many different search engines available. They all work basically the same: You type the word or phrase you want to find and click the Search button. The search engine then displays matches. (You also can fine-tune the search using different search options.)

The search tools differ in how they search—where they look for matches for your words. That means the results will vary. Also, how the results are displayed varies. Some display a short description. Some include some indication of how well the listed site matches the criteria you entered. Some may provide reviews of sites.

Follow these steps to search the Internet:

1. Click the Search button in your browser's toolbar. You see a list of the different search engines from which you can select.

2. In the text box, type the word or phrase you want to find and then click the Search button. (The name of the button will vary depending on which search engine you use.) You see the results of the search—a list of possible matches.

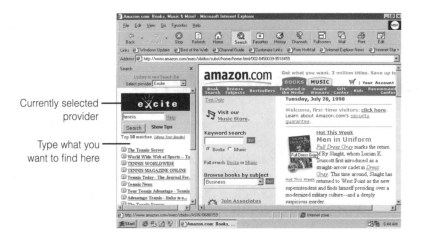

Currently selected
provider

Type what you
want to find here

3. To go to any of the found sites, click the link to that site. If additional sites were found, you can also display the next set of sites. Look for a link at the end of the list to display the next set of matches.

Search results

Beyond Survival

**Using a
Different
Search Tool**

If you don't find the topic you want, you can try a different search engine; the results may be different. You can display a list of search engines by clicking the Select provider drop-down list and then selecting the tool you want to use.

292

You can also go directly to a search site and then use any of the available tools. Here are the addresses of some popular search tools:

Excite	www.excite.com
Yahoo!	www.yahoo.com
Infoseek	www.infoseek.com
Lycos	www.lycos.com

Browsing a Search Directory

Many search engines include features to help you navigate among the vast amount of information. Many provide directories or channels. You can browse these channels to find topics of interest.

For instance, Infoseek, one of the most popular search engines, includes the following topics: Automotive, Business, Careers, Education, Health, Kids & Family, and others. When you select this search tool, these categories are displayed. (You can also select these categories and more from the Infoseek page.)

Infoseek, along with other search engines, provides a list of categories from which you can select a topic

To view the sites in these categories, click the link. You see sites within that category; click any of the links to go to that site.

Cheat Sheet

Starting Your Email Program

1. Log on to your Internet service provider.
2. Start the mail program.

Checking Your Mail

1. Start your email program.
2. Check for new messages.
3. To read a message, double-click it.

Responding to Mail

1. Display the message to which you want to reply.
2. Click the Reply button or select the Reply command. (The name of this command will vary from program to program.)
3. Type your response and click the Send button.

Sending New Mail

1. In your email program, click the New Message button. (The name of this button will vary from program to program.)
2. In the To text box, type the address of the recipient.
3. Type a short description or header for the message in the Subject field.
4. Click in the message area and type your message.
5. To send the message, click the Send button.

55

Sending and Receiving Email

If you are connected to the Internet, you can send messages to colleagues, clients, friends, and family, and you can read and reply to messages others send you. To use the email features of the Internet, you need to have a program that can handle email. You may use the program provided by your Internet service provider, or you may use the integrated email programs included with Microsoft's Internet Explorer (Outlook Express Mail) or Netscape Communicator (Netscape Messenger). As another alternative, you may use an online service such as America Online for your mail. Finally, you may purchase and use another email package.

Most email programs offer comparable features and work in a similar fashion. The exact steps you follow to access mail and send and receive mail will vary from program to program. This chapter uses Outlook Express as the mail program.

Basic Survival

Starting Your Email Program

To check your mail, you first log on to your Internet service provider and then start the mail program. The process will vary depending on which program you use. Usually you start the mail program as you do any other program: with a command or program icon.

When you install your email program, that program may put an icon on the desktop. You can double-click this icon to start your mail program.

If you aren't sure, check the information you received from your service provider.

After you start your mail program, you see the program window. The following figure shows the mail window for Outlook Express. If you use another program, your mail program will look a little differently, but should contain similar features.

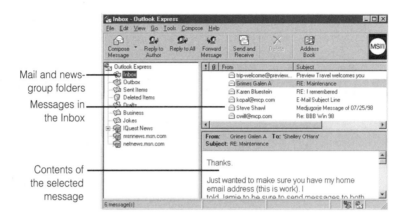

Mail and news-group folders

Messages in the Inbox

Contents of the selected message

Expect to find a menu bar with commands for accessing all the mail features. Most programs also include a toolbar with buttons you can use as shortcuts to common tasks like checking mail or creating a new message.

Most programs list the message headers in the window. This line tells you the sender, subject, and receive date. You can also usually tell which messages have been read and which have not. For instance, in Outlook Express, bold messages haven't been read.

The program window may be divided into panes, like Outlook Express. The left pane lists the folders for handling and storing mail (and also newsgroups). The top-right pane contains message headers, and the bottom-right pane displays the contents of the selected message.

Under-standing Your Email Address

To receive mail, you must have an email address, and this address is assigned to you by your Internet service provider. Usually you can select your username, which often is the first part of your email address. Here's an example of an address:

username@domain.net

The first part is a username, and the second part defines the server or Internet provider where the mail is sent. Again, check the information sent to you by your ISP to find out your email address.

Checking Your Mail

To check your mail, start the email program, check the mail, and then review any messages in your Inbox. Here are the basic steps:

1. Start your email program.

2. Check for new messages. Some programs may check automatically when you start the program. For others, you may have to select a command (or click a shortcut button) to check the mail. You may also have to type a password.

   Your mail program collects all the messages on your mail server and displays them in your Inbox.

3. To read a message, double-click it. You see the contents of the message in a separate message window.

The message window usually includes buttons and commands for handling the message (covered later in this chapter)

Responding to Mail

You can easily respond to a message you've received. Most programs complete the address and subject lines for you; you can then simply type the response. Follow these steps:

1. Display the message to which you want to reply.

2. Click the Reply button or select the Reply command. (The name of this command will vary from program to program.) You see a message reply window. When you reply, the address information is complete. The reply may also contain the text of the original message.

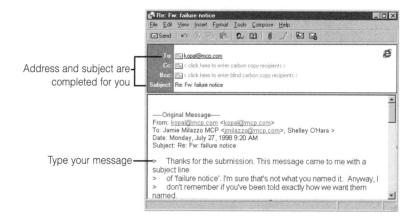

Address and subject are completed for you

Type your message

3. Type your response and click the Send button to send the reply.

Sending New Mail

You aren't limited to just responding to mail you receive. You can also send an email message to any person with an address. Follow these steps:

1. In your email program, click the New Message button. (The name of this button will vary from program to program.) You can also use a menu command. In Outlook Express, select Compose, New Message. You see a new message window.

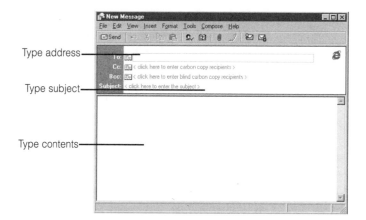

Type address

Type subject

Type contents

2. In the To text box, type the address of the recipient. You can also send a carbon copy and blind carbon copy to other recipients by entering addresses in these fields.

3. Type a short description or header for the message in the Subject field.

4. Click in the message area and type your message.

5. To send the message, click the Send button.

You may have other options for sending, depending on the program you are using. For instance, you can assign a priority to the message, attach a file, request a return receipt, and so on.

Beyond Survival

Handling Mail

When you receive a message, you have several choices of what to do with the message:

- Read and close the message. To close the message and keep it in your Inbox, click the Close (×) button for the message window.

- Reply to the message. Use the Reply to Author or Reply to Group buttons.

- Print the message. To print the message, look for a Print button in the toolbar or a Print command in the File menu.

- Delete the message. To delete the message, use the Delete button in the toolbar.

- Forward the message. To forward the message to another person, click the Forward button or use the Forward command. In the To text box, type the address of that person and then click the Send button.

Cheat Sheet

Subscribing to Newsgroups

1. Start your newsreader program.
2. Click the Newsgroups button or open the Tools menu and select Newsgroups. (The button you click and the command you select will vary if you are using a different program. Look for something similar.)
3. Select the news server you want to use.
4. In the newsgroups list, click the newsgroup you want to join and click the Subscribe button.
5. Continue subscribing to the newsgroups of interest.
6. When you've added all the newsgroups you want, click OK.

Reading Newsgroup Messages

1. From the news window, select the newsgroup you want to review.
2. To read a message, click the name in the list.

Replying to a Message

1. To reply to an existing message, select that message in the newsreader window.
2. Click the Reply to Group button. (The name of the button will vary. You also can use a menu command.)
3. Click in the message area and type your reply.
4. Click the Post Message button to post the message.

Posting a New Message

1. In the newsreader window, select the group to which you want to post the message.
2. Click the New Message button (or a similarly named button).
3. Type a subject in the Subject line.
4. Click in the message area and type your message.
5. Click the Post Message button.

56

Joining Newsgroups

A newsgroup is an online discussion group. Each newsgroup is devoted to a particular topic, and you can find newsgroups on topics ranging from current events to Elvis sightings, from engineering to classical music. There are thousands and thousands of newsgroups. The collection of all newsgroups is known as *Usenet.*

You can subscribe to newsgroups of interest and then review and post messages to join in this online discussion. To subscribe to and review newsgroup postings, you need a newsreader. You may have received a newsreader program from your Internet service provider. Alternatively, you can use the newsreader included with Internet Explorer (Outlook Express News) or Netscape Communicator (Netscape Collabra).

You don't pay a fee to subscribe to a newsgroup.

Basic Survival

Subscribing to Newsgroups

To read the messages and participate in the newsgroup, you subscribe to the groups you want. The process will vary from one program to another, but here are the steps for Outlook Express:

1. Start your newsreader program. To start Outlook Express, click Start, Programs, and Outlook Express.

2. Select your newsreader in the mail window.

3. Click the Newsgroups button or open the Tools menu and select Newsgroups. (The button you click and command you select will vary if you are using a different program. Look for something similar.)

4. Select the news server you want to use. You may be able to choose from several news servers. You should see the newsgroups in that server listed.

If this is the first time you are subscribing, you may be prompted to download the complete list. You can also display All Newsgroups or All New Newsgroups using the buttons in the dialog box.

Select newsgroup from this list...

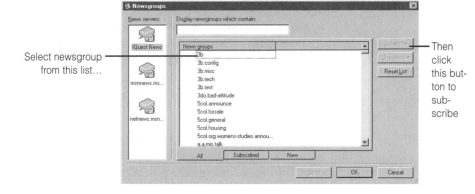

Then click this button to subscribe

5. In the newsgroups list, click the newsgroup you want to join and click the Subscribe button.

6. Continue subscribing to the newsgroups of interest.

7. When you've added all the newsgroups you want, click OK.

Reading Newsgroup Messages

After you have subscribed to a newsgroup, you can review any of the posted messages. Follow these steps:

1. From the news window, select the newsgroup you want to review. In Outlook Express, the newsgroups are listed in the left pane of the window. (You may have to expand the listing to see all the groups within a certain news server.) To select the newsgroup you want, click it.

Outlook Express retrieves the messages. Messages that have replies posted to them are marked with a plus sign. You can expand this list to see all the replies by clicking the plus sign.

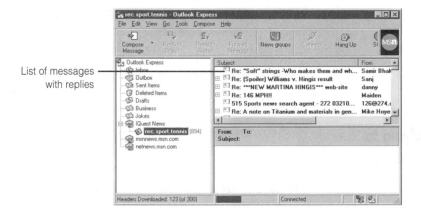

List of messages with replies

2. To read a message, click the name in the list. You see the message.

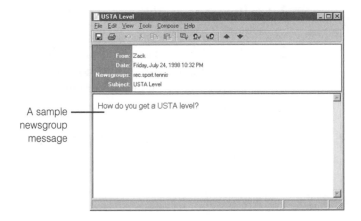

A sample newsgroup message

You can review other messages, select other newsgroups, post replies (covered next), or exit the program. To exit, click the Close (×) button for the newsreader.

When you are reviewing messages, keep in mind that messages are often replies from a previous posting. You may not understand the message you are reviewing because you haven't seen the earlier messages. It's kind of like walking in on the middle of a conversation. If the earlier messages aren't posted, you have to kind of guess the gist of the message in some cases.

Also, don't expect to find top-notch quality writing or comments in every postings. You might find that you have to spend some time finding a "good" conversation.

The messages in these newsgroups aren't screened for objectionable content. If you find something offensive, the best thing to do is just unsubscribe from that newsgroup.

Replying to a Message

Reviewing posted messages will give you an idea of the content and participants in a newsgroup. You may want to lurk around, reading messages, to get a feel for the atmosphere. Then when you are ready, you can post your own replies. Again, the steps will vary depending on which newsreader you use, but the basic process is similar.

Follow these steps to post a reply to an existing message using Outlook Express News:

1. To reply to an existing message, select that message in the newsreader window.

2. Click the Reply to Group button. (The name of the button will vary. You also can use a menu command.) You see a reply window with the contents of the original posting; the newsgroup is already completed for the To field.

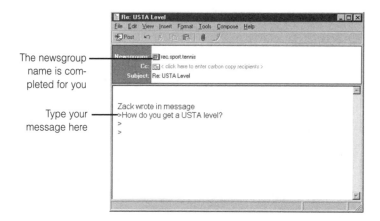

The newsgroup name is completed for you

Type your message here

3. Click in the message area and type your reply.

4. Click the Post Message button to post the message.

Beyond Survival

Posting a New Message

You aren't limited to joining existing "conversations." When a new message is posted, it starts a thread, and all responses are part of this thread. You can start your own thread by posting a new message. Follow these steps to post a new message to a newsgroup:

1. In the newsreader window, select the group to which you want to post the message.

2. Click the New Message button (or a similarly named button). You can also look for a New Message command. You see a new message window, with the current newsgroup entered in the To field.

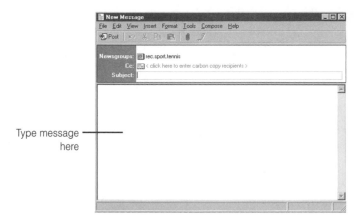

Type message here

3. Type a subject in the Subject line. This line will identify your message in the newsgroup window, so use something descriptive.

4. Click in the message area and type your message.

5. Click the Post Message button. The message is posted to the newsgroup for others to read and reply to.

If you change your mind about posting a message, you can cancel the message if you have not already clicked Post. Simply click the message's Close button and, when prompted, click the Yes button to confirm that you don't want to save the message. If you have already clicked the Post button, you cannot stop the message.

Index

A

accessibility options, 215
customizing, 216-217
displaying, 215
Accessibility Properties
dialog box, 215
Active Desktop
channels
displaying, 190, 192,
194
subscribing, 190, 193
deactivating, 192
displaying, 190-192
Add New Hardware
wizard, 254, 256-257
Add/Remove Programs
icon
programs
installing, 44-46
uninstalling, 46-47
installing components,
47-49
Add/Remove Programs
Properties dialog box,
234
adding
folders, Start menu, 54
Internet sites, Favorites
List, 284, 288
programs
Start menu, 50-52
Startup folder, 36
scheduled tasks, 258-260
text boxes (Paint), 98

addresses
email, 296
Internet (URLs)
browsing Internet, 284,
286
defined, 286
Airbrush tool (Paint), 94,
96
anti-virus programs, 264,
267 See also Norton Anti-
Virus
applications See programs
Arrange (All) command
(Window menu), 74, 77
Arrange Icons command
(desktop shortcut menu),
22, 24
arranging
desktop icons, 22, 24
windows, 21
associated programs, file
types, 160
associating sounds with
events, 210, 212, 214
audio
CDs (music)
different tracks, playing,
107
information (artist, title,
tracks) entering, 106
playing, 102-104
sounds
associating with events,
210, 212, 214
playing, 102, 104,
210-212, 214

recording, 107-108
schemes, 210, 212-213

B

background (desktop)
patterns
editing, 180-181
selecting, 174, 176
wallpaper
images as, 179-180
selecting, 174-176
tiling, 176
backups
all files, 236-238
Backup utility, 237
devices, 238
naming, 238
restoring files, 242, 244,
246
backup set, 244
location, 245
restoration device, 244
selected files, 236,
239-240
storage media, 238
borders (windows), 20
browsing Internet, 285
links, 284-285
toolbar buttons, 287
URLs (addresses), 284,
286
Brush tool (Paint), 94, 96
buttons
CD Player, 107

Command dialog boxes, 12, 16
mouse, 204-206
Option dialog boxes, 12, 16

C

calculations (mathematical), 120-121
Calculator
figuring calculations, 120-121
modes, 120
opening, 120-121
values, 122
Cancel Printing command (Document menu), 248, 251
canceling print jobs, 248, 251
Cascade command (taskbar shortcut menu), 21
CD Player
buttons, 107
CDs (audio)
information (artist, title, tracks) entering, 106
launching, 102-103
playing, 103-104, 107
CD Player: Disc Settings dialog box, 106
CDs (audio)
information (artist, title, tracks), entering, 106
playing, 102-104, 107
cell ranges, 60, 62
changing
Calculator modes, 120
file and folder window views, 130, 132
file types, 73

icons appearance, 174, 177-178
Internet connection settings, 282-283
scheduled tasks, 258, 261, 263
channels (Active Desktop)
displaying, 190, 192, 194
subscribing, 190, 193
check boxes (dialog boxes), 12, 15
checking email, 294, 297
cleaning up disks, 228-230
options, 228, 230-231
selecting files, 229
clearing Calculator values, 122
clock, 199
Close command (File menu), 78-79
Close Program dialog box, 6
closing
documents, 78-79
menus (programs), 14
programs, 20, 32, 34
windows, 20
clusters (hard disks), 225
colors
Paint objects, 99
schemes
creating, 181-182
saving, 182
selecting, 174, 177
Command button (dialog boxes), 12, 16
commands
Arrange Icons (desktop shortcut menu), 22, 24
Document menu, 248, 251
Edit menu
Copy, 64, 67, 88, 90, 152

Cut, 64, 66, 88, 90, 152
Paste, 64, 67, 69, 88, 90, 152
Paste Special, 69, 152
Undo, 150
File menu
Close, 78-79
Exit, 32, 34
New, 78-79
Open, 74-75, 124, 126
Page Setup, 82, 84, 92
Print, 82-83, 88, 90
Print Preview, 82, 84
Save, 70-72, 88, 108, 124-126
Save As, 70, 72-73
Format menu, 92
Paint menus, 98
Printer menu, 248, 251
programs, keyboard shortcuts, 16
Programs (Start menu), 10, 32, 95
Accessories, 88-89, 102-105, 110-111, 114, 120-121, 124
installing programs, 47
launching programs, 32, 36
Windows Explorer, 130, 134
Search menu, 124, 127
selecting
programs, 12, 14
Start menu, 12-13
Settings (Start menu), 10, 130, 132, 135
Control Panel, 42, 44, 46, 48
Folder Options, 160
shortcut menu
Create Shortcut(s) Here, 56, 58

Delete, 56, 59
Rename, 56, 58
shortcut menus
selecting, 16-17
Start menu, 10-11
Documents, 10, 32
Favorites, 10
Find, 11
Find, Files or Folders,
162-164, 166
Help, 11
Programs,
Run, 11, 32, 47
Shut Down, 11
taskbar shortcut menu
Cascade, 21
Tile Horizontally, 21
Tile Vertically, 21
Window menu, 74, 77
components (programs),
42, 47-49
composing faxes, 111-113
connection settings
(Internet), 282-283
contextual menus *See*
shortcut menus
Control Panel, 42, 44, 46,
48
Copy command (Edit
menu), 64, 67, 88, 90,
152
copying
data, another program,
68-69
files, 149
between folders, 148,
150
commands, 152
to floppy disks, 148,
151
folders, 138, 142
Paint objects, 100
text, 64, 67

Create Shortcut dialog box,
51
Create Shortcut(s) Here
command (shortcut
menu), 56, 58
Curve tool (Paint), 94, 96
Cut command (Edit
menu), 64, 66, 88, 90,
152
cutting and pasting text,
64, 66

D

data
copying, another
program, 68-69
pasting as objects, 69
date, 200-202
default printer, 252
defragmenting hard drive,
224-227
Delete command (shortcut
menu), 56, 59
deleting
files, 154-155
folders, 138, 141, 155
objects (Paint), 98
programs, 42, 46-47
Start menu, 50, 53-54
Startup folder, 37
scheduled tasks, 258, 261
shortcut icons, 35
shortcuts, 56, 59
text, 64-65
deselecting files, 144
desktop (Windows), 5-6, 9
Active
channels, 190, 192-194
deactivating, 192
displaying, 190-192
colors

schemes, 181-182
selecting, 174, 177
setting individually,
181-182
icons, 9-10
appearance, 174,
177-178
arranging, 22, 24
lining up, 25
My Computer *See* My
Computer icon
Network
Neighborhood, 10
Recycle Bin *See* Recycle
Bin
patterns
editing, 180-181
selecting, 174, 176
regional settings, 200,
202-203
screen size, 178-179
screen savers
options, 187-188
passwords, 184,
186-187
previewing, 185
selecting, 184-186
stopping, 184, 186
Start button, 10
taskbar, 11
date, 200-202
displaying, 50-51,
53-55
moving, 196-197
options, 196, 198-199
sizing, 196, 198
switching between
programs, 11, 38
time, 200-202
troubleshooting, not
displaying, 5-6
wallpaper
images as, 179-180

selecting, 174-176
tiling, 176
desktop shortcut menu
commands, Arrange
Icons, 22, 24
Device Manager, 264-266
dialing phone numbers
(Phone Dialer), 114
dialog boxes, 259 *See also*
wizards
Accessibility Properties,
215
Add/Remove Programs
Properties, 234
CD Player: Disc Settings,
106
Close Program, 6
Create Shortcut, 51
Disk Cleanup, 231
Display Properties, 175
features, 12
Folder Options, 135
Format, 233
Keyboard Properties, 206
Mouse Properties, 205
Open, 75, 102, 104-105
options, 12, 15-16
Page Setup, 92
Print, 83
Remove Shortcuts/Folder,
53
Run, 47
Save As, 71-73, 108
Shut Down Windows, 4
Sounds Properties, 211
Taskbar Properties,
50-51, 53-55
directories (search engines),
293
Disk Cleanup dialog box,
231
disk icons, 22-23

disks
clusters, 225
floppy, 232-234
hard
cleaning up, 228-231
defragmenting, 224-227
errors, correcting,
220-221, 223
properties, 168, 171
startup, 232-235
Display Properties dialog
box, 175
displaying
accessibility options, 215
Active Desktop, 190-192
associated programs, file
types, 160
CD Player: Disc Settings
dialog box, 106
channels (Active
Desktop), 190, 192,
194
clock, 199
Control Panel, 42, 44,
46, 48
defragmenting process,
224, 227
documents (all open), 74,
77
faxes, 110, 113-114
files and folders
icons, 174, 177-178
My Computer icon, 172
Open dialog box, 75,
102, 104-105
Page Setup dialog box, 92
Print dialog box, 83
print jobs, 248-251
properties
disks, 168, 171
files and folders,
168-170
system, 168, 172

Remove
Shortcuts/Folder
dialog box, 53
Run dialog box, 47
Save As dialog box,
71-73, 108
shortcut menus, 16-17
Start menu, 10
submenus, 13
submenus, 12
taskbar (desktop), 50-51,
53-55
Taskbar Properties dialog
box, 54
document icons, 22-23
Document menu
commands, Cancel
Printing, 248, 251
documents
closing, 78-79
creating, 78-79
displaying (all open), 74,
77
formatting features, 82,
84
opening, 32, 34, 74-75
previewing (before print-
ing), 82, 84
printing, 82-83
previewing (before
printing), 82, 84
WordPad, 88, 90
saving, 70, 72
another file type, 73
another name, 70, 72
first time, 70-72
WordPad, 88
switching between, 74,
76
Documents command
(Start menu), 10, 32

dragging window borders, 20

dragging and dropping files, 148-150

drawing objects (Paint), 97

drop-down list boxes (dialog boxes), 12, 15

E

Edit menu commands
Copy, 64, 67, 88, 90, 152
Cut, 64, 66, 88, 90, 152
Paste, 64, 67, 69, 88, 90, 152
Paste Special, 69
Undo, 150
editing
text (WordPad), 88, 90
text files, 124, 126
Ellipses tool (Paint), 94, 96
email, 295
addresses, 296
checking, 294, 297
programs, 294-296
receiving, 299
responding, 294, 297-298
sending, 294, 298-299
emptying Recycle Bin, 154, 156-157
entering text (WordPad), 88-89
Eraser/Color Eraser tool (Paint), 94, 96
erasing parts of objects (Paint), 98
errors (hard disks), 220-221, 223
events (sounds), 210, 212, 214

Excite Web site, 293

Exit command (File menu), 32, 34

exiting programs, 32, 34

Explorer, 130, 134

extensions, filenames, 160

F

Favorites command (Start menu), 10

Favorites List, 284, 288

faxes
receiving and displaying, 110, 113-114
sending, 110-113
figuring calculations, 120-121
File menu commands
Close, 78-79
Exit, 32, 34
New, 78-79
Open, 74-75, 124, 126
Page Setup, 82, 84, 92
Print, 82-83, 88, 90
Print Preview, 82, 84
Save, 70-72, 88, 108, 124-126
Save As, 70, 72-73
files
associated programs, 160
backups
all files, 236-238
selected files, 236, 239-240
cleaning up, 228-230
options, 228, 230-231
selecting files, 229
copying, 149
between folders, 148, 150
commands, 152

to floppy disks, 148, 151
deleting, 154-155
deselecting, 144
displaying
My Computer icon, 130-131
Windows Explorer, 130, 134
dragging and dropping, 148-150
finding
by content, 162, 164-165
by date, 162, 166
by name, 162-164
moving commands, 152
names
extensions, 160
non acceptable characters, 159
properties, 168-169
renaming, 158-160
restoring, 242, 246
backup set, 244
location, 245
restoration device, 244
rows, 144-145
selecting, 144, 146-147
text
creating, 124
editing, 124, 126
fonts, 126
inserting time/date, 126
opening, 124, 126
searching for text, 124, 127
playable, 105
types, 73
window contents
sorting, 130, 133
views, changing, 130, 132

Fill With Color tool (Paint), 94, 96
filling Paint objects, color, 99
Find command (Start menu), 11
Find command (Search menu), 124, 127
Find, Files or Folders command (Start menu), 162-164, 166
Find Setup Wizard, 29
finding
  files and folders
    by content, 162, 164-165
    by date, 162, 166
    by name, 162-164
  help topics
    by searching, 26, 29-30
    help index, 26, 28-29
    help table of contents, 26-28
floppy disks, 232-234
folder icons, 22-23
Folder Options dialog box, 135
folders, 131
  adding, Start menu, 54
  copying, 138, 142
  creating, 138-139
  deleting, 138, 141, 155
  displaying
    My Computer icon, 130-131
    Windows Explorer, 130, 134
  finding
    by content, 162, 164-165
    by date, 162, 166
    by name, 162-164
  moving, 138, 141-142
  names, 159

properties, 168, 170
renaming, 138, 140
Start menu, creating, 52
Startup
  adding programs, 36
  deleting programs, 37
window contents
  sorting, 130, 133
  views, changing, 130, 132
fonts, 126
Format dialog box, 233
Format menu commands, 92
formatting
  disks, 232-234
  Word Pad
    pages, 92
    paragraphs, 91
    text, 88, 90-92
Free-Form Select tool (Paint), 94, 96
Freecell, 116

G-H

games
  Freecell, 116
  Hearts, 116, 118
  Minesweeper, 119
  Solitaire, 116-117
hard disks
  cleaning up, 228-230
    options, 228, 230-231
    selecting files, 229
  clusters, 225
  defragmenting, 224-227
  errors, correcting, 220-221, 223
hardware, installing, 255
Hearts, 116, 118
help topics, finding
  by searching, 26, 29-30

help index, 26, 28-29
help table of contents, 26-28
Help command (Start menu), 11
hiding taskbar, 199
history list, Internet, 284, 289

I-J

icons
  Add/Remove Programs
    installing components (programs), 47-49
    installing programs, 44-46
    uninstalling programs, 46-47
  defined, 9-10
  desktop, 9-10
    appearance, 174, 177-178
    arranging, 22, 24
    lining up, 25
  My Computer See My Computer icon
  Network Neighborhood, 10
  Recycle Bin See Recycle Bin
  disks, 22-23
  documents, 22-23
  folders, 22-23
  moving, 22, 24
  programs, 22-23
  shortcut, 22, 24, 32, 35
  Start menu, 199
  types, 22-24
Image, Clear Image command (Paint menu), 98
images as wallpaper, 179-180

Infoseek Web site, 293
installing
    hardware, 255
        Add New Hardware
            wizard, 254, 256-257
        Plug and Play, 255-256
    printers, 248-250
    programs, 42
        Add/Remove Programs
            icon, 44-46
        components, 42, 47-49
        Run command, 47
IntelliPoint mouse, 205
Internet
    browsing, 285
        links, 284-285
        toolbar buttons, 287
        URLs (addresses), 284,
            286
    connection
        requirements, 273-274
        settings, changing,
            282-283
    email, 295
        addresses, 296
        checking, 294, 297
        programs, 294-296
        receiving, 299
        responding, 294,
            297-298
        sending, 294, 298-299
    Favorites List, 284, 288
    history list, 284, 289
    logging on and off,
        280-282
    newsgroups
        defined, 301
        posting messages, 300,
            305
        reading messages, 300,
            302-303
        replying to messages,
            300, 304

subscribing, 300-302
        Usenet, 301
    searching, 290-293
    setup, 272, 274-278, 279
    URLs, 286
Internet Explorer
    Connection Wizard, 272,
        274, 279
inverting file selections,
    147
ISPs (Internet service
    providers), 273

K-L

keyboard
    accessibility options,
        216-217
    properties, 206
    restarting Windows 98, 6
    selecting text, 60, 62
    shortcuts
        closing documents,
            78-79
        program commands, 16
        program menus, 16
        switching between open
            programs, 38-39
Keyboard Properties dialog
    box, 206
launching
    Calculator, 120-121
    Explorer, 130, 134
    Phone Dialer, 114
    text files, 126
    windows, 19
    CD Player, 102-103
    documents, 32, 24,
        74-75
    email programs, 294-295
    Internet Explorer
        Connection Wizard,
            272, 274, 279

Internet sites, Favorites
    List, 284, 288
Media Player, 102, 105
NotePad, 124
Outlook Express, 301
Paint, 95
programs
    at startup, 36
    opening documents, 32,
        34
    Run command, 32, 36
    shortcut icons, 32, 35
    Start menu, 32-33
    Sound Recorder, 102,
        104
    Windows 98, 2-3
    WordPad, 88-89
Line tool (Paint), 94, 96
lining up desktop icons, 25
links, 284-285
list boxes (dialog boxes),
    12, 15
list of ISPs Web site, 274
logging on and off
    Internet, 280-282

M

Magnifier tool (Paint), 94,
    96
maintenance
    backups
        all files, 236-238
        selected files, 236,
            239-240
        storage media, 238
    cleaning up disks,
        228-230
        options, 228, 230-231
        selecting files, 229
    defragmenting hard drive,
        224-227
    Device Manager, 264-266

formatting disks,
232-234
restoring files, 242, 244,
246
backup set, 244
location, 245
restoration device, 244
ScanDisk, 220-221, 223
scheduled tasks
adding, 258-260
deleting, 258, 261
modifying, 258, 261,
263
startup disks
creating, 232-235
defined, 234
viruses, avoiding, 264,
267-269
maximizing windows, 20
McAfee Web site, 267
media clips, 102, 105-106
Media Player
launching, 102, 105
video files, 105-106
menus
programs
closing, 14
keyboard shortcuts, 16
shortcut commands,
16-17
Start
adding folders, 54
adding programs, 50-52
commands, 10-11,
12-13
deleting programs, 50,
53-54
displaying, 10
Documents command,
10
Favorites command, 10
Find command, 11
Help command, 11

launching programs,
32-33
Programs command, 10
rearranging, 55
Run command, 11
Settings command, 10
Shut Down command,
11
Microsoft Fax, 111-113
Minesweeper, 119
minimizing
programs, 38, 40
windows, 20, 38, 40
modems, 273
modes (Calculator), 120
modulator-demodulator,
273
mouse
buttons, 204-206
IntelliPoint, 205
pointers
accessibility options,
217
changing, 204, 207
speed, 204, 207-208
trails, 204, 207-208
selecting text, 60-61
Mouse Properties dialog
box, 205
movies, playing, 102,
105-106
moving
files, 148-150, 152
folders, 138, 141-142
icons, 22, 24
taskbar, 196-197
text, 64-65
windows, 21
multimedia, 103
music CDs.
information (artist, title,
tracks), entering, 106
playing, 102-104, 107

My Computer icon, 9
disk properties, 168, 171
displaying, 172
files and folders, 130-131
system properties, 168,
172

N

names files and folders,
159
Network Neighborhood
icon, 10
New command (File
menu), 78-79
newsgroups
defined, 301
messages
posting, 300, 305
reading, 300, 302-303
replying, 300, 304
subscribing, 300-302
Usenet, 301
Norton Anti-Virus, 264,
268-269
NotePad
launching, 124
text files
creating, 124
editing, 124, 126
fonts, 126
inserting time/date, 126
opening, 124, 126

O

objects (Paint)
copying, 100
deleting, 98
drawing, 97
erasing parts, 98

Open command (File menu), 74-75, 124, 126
Open dialog box, 75, 102, 104-105
opening *See* launching
Option button (dialog boxes), 12, 16
Outlook Express, 301

P-Q

Page Setup command (File menu), 82, 84, 92
Page Setup dialog box, 92
pages (WordPad), formatting, 92
Paint
launching, 95
objects
copying, 100
deleting, 98
drawing, 97
erasing parts, 98
filling with color, 99
Rectangle, 94, 96
text boxes, 98
tools (listing of), 94-96
Paint menu commands, Image, Clear Image, 98
Paragraph command (Format menu), 92
paragraphs (WordPad), formatting, 91
passwords (screen savers), 184, 186-187
Paste command (Edit menu), 64, 67, 69, 88, 90, 152
Paste Special command (Edit menu), 69
pasting data as objects, 69
patterns (desktop)

editing, 180-181
selecting, 174, 176
pausing print jobs, 248, 251
Pencil tool (Paint), 94, 96
Phone Dialer, 114
phone numbers, dialing, 114
Pick Color tool (Paint), 94, 96
playing
CDs (audio), 102-104, 107
Freecell, 116
Hearts, 116, 118
media clips, 102, 105-106
Minesweeper, 119
Solitaire, 116-117
sounds, 102, 104, 210-212, 214
Plug and Play, 255-256
pointers (mouse)
accessibility options, 217
changing, 204, 207
speed, 204, 207-208
trails, 204, 207-208
Polygon tool (Paint), 94, 96
posting newsgroup messages, 300, 305
previewing documents (before printing), 82, 84
Print command (File menu), 82-83, 88, 90
Print dialog box, 83
print jobs, 248, 251
Print Preview command (File menu), 82, 84
Printer menu, Pause Printing command, 248, 251

printers
default, 252
installing, 248-250
printing documents, 82-83
previewing (before printing), 82, 84
WordPad, 88, 90
program icons, 22-23
programs, 12
adding
Start menu, 50-52
Startup folder, 36
closing, 20
commands
keyboard shortcuts, 16
selecting, 12, 14
deleting, 42, 46-47
Start menu, 50, 53-54
Startup folder, 37
exiting, 32, 34
installing, 42
Add/Remove Programs icon, 44-46
components, 47-49
Run command, 47
launching
at startup, 36
opening documents, 32, 34
Run command, 32, 36
shortcut icons, 32, 35
Start menu, 32-33
menus
closing, 14
keyboard shortcuts, 16
Microsoft Fax, 111-113
minimizing, 38, 40
Paint *See* Paint
purchasing, 43-44
switching between, 11, 38-39
Programs command (Start menu), 10, 32, 95

Programs, Accessories command (Start menu), 88-89, 102-105, 110-111, 114, 120-121, 124
properties
disks, 168, 171
files and folders, 168-170
icons, 174, 177-178
keyboard, 206
system, 168, 172
purchasing programs, 43-44

R

ranges (cells), 60, 62
reading
newsgroup messages, 300, 302-303
Start menu, 55
receiving
email, 299
faxes, 110, 113-114
recording sounds, 107-108
Rectangle tool (Paint), 94, 96
Recycle Bin, 9
deleted items, retrieving, 154, 156
emptying, 154, 156-157
regional settings, 200, 202-203
Remove Shortcuts/Folder dialog box, 53
Rename command (shortcut menu), 56, 58
renaming
files, 158-160
folders, 138, 140
shortcuts, 56, 58

replying, newsgroup messages, 300, 304
resizing
taskbar, 196, 198
windows, 20
resolution, 178-179
responding, email, 294, 297-298
restarting Windows 98, 2, 4-6
restoring
files, 242, 246
backup set, 244
location, 245
restoration device, 244
maximized windows, 20
retrieving deleted items, Recycle Bin, 154, 156
Rounded Rectangle tool (Paint), 94, 96
rows, files, 144-145
Run command (Start menu), 11, 32, 47
installing programs, 47
launching programs, 32, 36
Run dialog box, 11, 32, 36, 47

S

Save As command (File menu), 70, 72-73
Save As dialog box, 71-73, 108
Save command (File menu), 70-72, 88, 108, 124-126
saving
color schemes, 182
documents, 70, 72
another file type, 73

another name, 70, 72
first time, 70-72
WordPad, 88
ScanDisk
options, 220, 223
running, 220-221, 223
Scheduled Task wizard, 259-260
scheduled tasks
adding, 258-260
changing, 258, 261, 263
deleting, 258, 261
screen (monitor)
accessibility options, 217
colors and size, 178-179
screen savers
options, 187-188
passwords, 184, 186-187
previewing, 185
selecting, 184-186
stopping, 184, 186
search engines, 291, 293
Search menu commands, Find, 124, 127
searching
for text, text files, 124, 127
help topics, 26, 29-30
Internet, 290-293
Select tool (Paint), 94, 96
selecting
color schemes, 174, 177
commands
programs, 12, 14
shortcut menu, 16-17
Start menu, 12-13
files, 144, 146
inverting, 147
rows, 144-145
fonts, text files, 126
formatting features, documents, 82, 84

multiple files, 144, 146
ranges (cells), 60, 62
   text
      keyboard, 60, 62
      mouse, 60-61
sending
   email, 294, 298-299
   faxes, 110-113
Settings command (Start
   menu), 10
   Control Panel, 42, 44,
      46, 48
   Folder Options, 130,
      132, 135, 160
   Taskbar & Start Menu,
      50-51, 53-55
shortcut menus
   commands
      Create Shortcut(s) Here,
         56, 58
      Delete, 56, 59
      Rename, 56, 58
      selecting, 16-17
   displaying, 16-17
shortcuts, 56, 58
   creating, 56-58
   deleting, 56, 59
   icons, 22, 24
      creating, 35
      deleting, 35
      launching programs, 32,
         35
   renaming, 56, 58
showing See displaying
Shut Down command
   (Start menu), 11
Shut Down Windows
   dialog box, 4
shutting down Windows
   98, 2, 4
sites (Web)
   Excite, 293
   Infoseek, 293

list of ISPs, 274
   McAfee, 267
   Symantec, 267
   Yahoo!, 293
Solitaire, 116-117
sorting window contents,
   files and folders, 130
Sound Recorder
   playing sounds, 104
   launching, 102, 104
   recording sounds,
      107-108
sounds See also audio
   associating with events,
      210, 212, 214
   playing, 102, 104,
      210-212, 214
   recording, 107-108
   schemes, 210, 212-213
Sounds Properties dialog
   box, 211
special needs users (accessibility options), 215
   customizing, 216-217
   displaying, 215
spin boxes (dialog boxes),
   12, 15
Start button, 10
Start menu
   commands, 10-11, 12-13
      See also Start menu
      commands
   displaying, 10
   Documents command,
      10
   Favorites command, 10
   Find command, 11
   folders, adding, 54
   Help command, 11
   icons, 199
   programs
      adding, 50-52
      deleting, 50, 53-54

   launching, 32-33
      Programs command,
         10
   rearranging, 55
   Run command, 11
   Settings command, 10
   Shut Down command,
      11
Start menu commands
   Documents, 32
   Find, Files or Folders,
      162-164, 166
   Programs, 32, 95
      Accessories, 88-89,
         102-105, 110-111,
         114, 120-121, 124
      Windows Explorer, 130,
         134
   Run, 32, 47
   Settings
      Control Panel, 42, 44,
         46, 48
      Folder Options, 130,
         132, 135, 160
      Taskbar & Start Menu,
         50-51, 53-55
starting See launching
startup programs, 36
startup disks
   creating, 232-235
   defined, 234
Startup folder
   adding programs, 36
   deleting programs, 37
StickyKeys, 217
storage
   backups, 238
   clusters, 225
storing Calculator values,
   122
submenus, 12-13
subscribing
   channels, 193

Office 97 Cheat Sheet

newsgroups, 300,
301-302
surfing *See* browsing
switching between
documents, 74, 76
programs, 11, 38-39
Symantec Web site, 267
system
properties, 168, 172
troubleshooting, not
responding, 4-5

T

tabs (dialog boxes), 12, 15
Tabs command (Format
menu), 92
taskbar (desktop), 11
date, 200-202
displaying, 50-51, 53-55
hiding, 199
moving, 196-197
options, 196, 198-199
sizing, 196, 198
switching between pro-
grams, 11, 38
time, 200-202
Taskbar Properties dialog
box, 54
taskbar shortcut menu
commands, 21
tasks (scheduled)
adding, 258-260
deleting, 258, 261
modifying, 258, 261, 263
templates, 80
text
copying, 64, 67
cutting and pasting, 64,
66
deleting, 64-65

files
creating, 124
editing, 124, 126
fonts, 126
inserting time/date, 126
opening, 124, 126
searching for text, 124,
127
moving, 64-65
selecting
keyboard, 60, 62
mouse, 60-61
WordPad
editing, 88, 90
entering, 88-89
formatting, 88, 90-92
text boxes
Paint, 98
dialog boxes, 12, 15
Text tool (Paint), 94, 96
Tile Horizontally com-
mand (taskbar shortcut
menu), 21
Tile Vertically command
(taskbar shortcut menu),
21
tiling wallpaper, 176
time, 200-202
toolbar buttons, browsing
Internet, 287
tools (Paint), 94-96
troubleshooting
avoiding viruses, 264,
267-269
desktop, not displaying,
5-6
Device Manager, 264-266
nothing happens at start-
up, 5

Start Menu won't open, 6
system not responding,
4-5

U-V

Undo command (Edit
menu), 150
Uniform Resource Locator
(URLs), 284, 286
uninstalling programs, 42,
46-47
URLs (Uniform Resource
Locator), 284, 286
Usenet, 301
values (Calculator), 122
video
media clips, 102, 105-
106
playable files, 105
viewing *See* displaying
viruses, avoiding, 264,
267-269
visual effects, icons, 174,
177-178

W-X-Y-Z

wallpaper
images as, 179-180
selecting, 174-176
tiling, 176
Web images as wallpaper,
179-180
Web pages, desktop as
(Active Desktop)
channels
displaying, 190, 192,
194
subscribing, 190, 193

deactivating, 192
displaying, 190-192
Web sites *See also* channels
Excite, 293
Infoseek, 293
list of ISPs, 274
McAfee, 267
Symantec, 267
Yahoo!, 293
Web view, 130, 135
Window menu commands,
Arrange (All), 74, 77
windows
arranging, 21
borders, 20
closing, 20
files and folders, contents,
130, 132-133
maximizing, 20
minimizing, 20, 38, 40
moving, 21
opening, 19
resizing, 20
Windows 98
restarting, 2, 4-6
launching, 2-3
shutting down, 2, 4
Windows Explorer, 130,
134
wizards, 259 *See also*
dialog boxes
Add New Hardware, 254,
256-257
Find Setup, 29
Internet Explorer
Connection, 272, 274,
279
Scheduled Task, 259-260
WordPad
documents, 88, 90
launching, 88-89

pages, formatting, 92
paragraphs, 91
text
editing, 88, 90
entering, 88-89
formatting, 88, 90-92
worksheet ranges, 60, 62
Yahoo! Web site, 293